# ARMIES OF THE F

*Text by*
MARK HEALY
*Colour plates by*
ANGUS McBRIDE

Published in 1992 by Osprey Publishing,
Elms Court, Chapel Way, Botley, Oxford
OX2 9LP, United Kingdom.

Also published as Elite 40: *New Kingdom Egypt*.

ISBN 1 85532 939 5

Filmset in Great Britain by Tradespools Ltd., Frome,
Somerset
Printed in China through World Print Ltd.

FOR A CATALOGUE OF ALL BOOKS PUBLISHED BY
OSPREY MILITARY, AUTOMOTIVE AND AVIATION
PLEASE WRITE TO:

The Marketing Manager, Osprey Direct USA,
32518 Dequindre, Warren, MI 48092, USA

The Marketing Manager, Osprey Direct UK,
PO Box 140, Wellingborough, Northants, NN8 4ZA,
United Kingdom

or visit Osprey's website at: *http://www.osprey-publishing.co.uk*

## Acknowledgements
Graphics reproduced with permission of Firebird
Books. First used in author's title 'Warriors of the Old
Testament' published by the same company.

FRONT COVER: 'Troop of Soldiers' by Nina Davis
(1947.30, Ashmolean Museum, Oxford)

# INTRODUCTION

It was in the latter part of the second millennium BC that the ancient Near East witnessed a prolonged and at times bitter contest between the great powers of the day as they vied for control and domination of the Eastern Mediterranean seaboard or Levant. While such a convergence of imperial ambitions, centred on the lands we know today as Syria and the Lebanon, reflects the shared perception of the vital economic importance of this area in ancient times, it cannot totally account for the prolonged interest of Hittite, Mitanni and Egypt in the region. This is certainly true of the latter power. The 'Kingdom of the Two Lands' had traditionally viewed the territories of the Levant as falling within its 'sphere of influence'.

However, the presence of Egyptian armies campaigning as far north as the River Euphrates between the 16th and 13th centuries BC, contesting control of such strategically important cities as Tunip and Kadesh (see map), against first the Kingdom of Mitanni and later the Hittites, must be seen as a radical departure from the military policies of the Old and Middle Kingdoms.

Such a historical divergence arose directly from a

*The ferocious wounds in the head of the mummy of the early 16th-century BC king Seqenenre Tao II indicate that he died in battle fighting the Hyksos. Analysis of the remains shows that the body was already in a state of decomposition by the time it was mummified, suggesting that it was recovered after having been abandoned on the battlefield. (C. el Mahdy)*

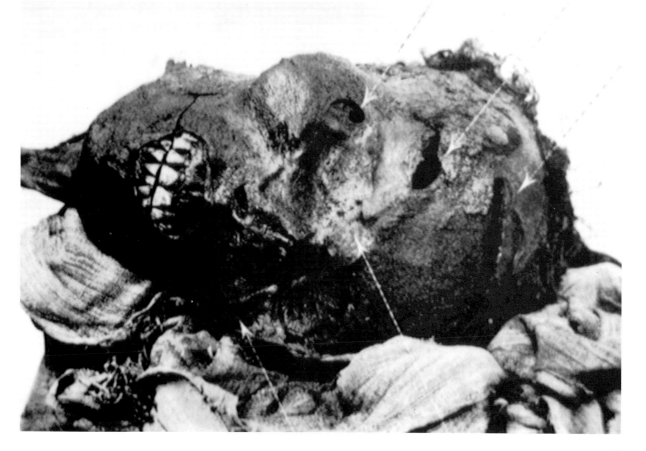

changed perception of Egypt's security needs following its century-long 'domination' at the hands of foreign rulers known as the Hyksos. This experience of foreign rule was seminal for the Egyptians in many ways. The principal consequence was, however, the transformation of Egypt into a military state by the pharaohs of the 18th Dynasty. The harnessing of the resources of the state and their use in the maintenance and deployment of a powerful standing army was directed towards the servicing of an aggressive foreign policy which saw the emergence of Egypt as a thoroughgoing imperialistic power. In a very real sense it was this translation of Egypt into a military state, with all that presaged on the international scene in the ancient Near East, that is the dominating, if not defining, feature of what is called the 'New Kingdom' period of her history.

# CHRONOLOGY

(The chronology that follows uses that employed in the third edition of the Cambridge Ancient History. All dates are BC.)

c1674 The Hyksos take control of Egypt.
**18th Dynasty**
c1570 Amosis becomes Pharaoh.
c1565 Amosis expels the Hyksos.
c1546–1526 Amenophis I leads possible campaign into Syria.
1525–c1512 Tuthmosis I engages forces of Kingdom of Mitanni near River Euphrates.
c1512–1504 Tuthmosis II.
1503–1482 Hatshepsut.
1504–1450 Tuthmosis III.
c1482 Battle of Megiddo. From 1482 Tuthmosis III led almost annual campaigns into Asia. Battles against Mitanni.
1450–1425 Amenophis II continues contest with Mitanni. Campaigns in Syria and Canaan.
1425–1417 Tuthmosis IV. Peace made with Mitanni.
1417–1379 Amenophis III.
1379–1362 Amenophis IV (Akhenaten). Eclipse of Mitanni. Rise of Neo-Hittite Empire under Suppiluliumas.

1364–1361 Smenkhkare.
1361–1352 Tutankhamun.
1352–1348 Ay.
1348–1320 Horemhab.
**19th Dynasty**
1320–1318 Ramasses I.
1318–1304 Seti I campaigns in Canaan and the Levant.
1304–1237 Ramasses II.
c1300 Battle of Qadesh.
c1284 Peace treaty between Egypt and the Hittites.
1236–1223 Merneptah.
1222–1200 Period of Turmoil.
**20th Dynasty**
1200–1198 Sethnakhte.
1198–1166 Ramasses III.
c1200 Invasion of 'Sea Peoples'. Collapse of Near Eastern political order.
1113–1085 Ramasses XI—end of New Kingdom.

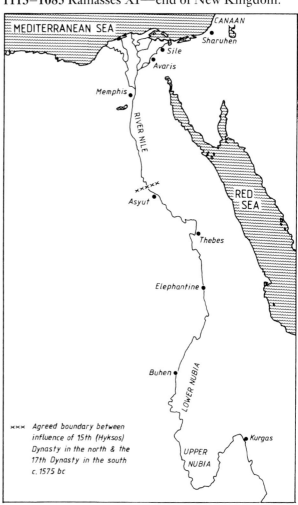

×̶×̶×̶ Agreed boundary between influence of 15th (Hyksos) Dynasty in the north & the 17th Dynasty in the south c.1575 bc

# THE RULE OF THE HYKSOS

Any understanding of Egyptian imperialism in the New Kingdom period must be founded on the native response to the experience of foreign rule during the Second Intermediate Period between 1640 and 1532 BC. The traditional image of the Hyksos descent on Egypt, in which the military superiority of these predominantly Semitic 'conquerors', symbolised by their employment of bronze weapons, chariots and composite bow, spreading fire and destruction before them and ruthlessly subjugating the 'Kingdom of the Two Lands', is still one that has attractions for many. In its simplicity, this account serves the desirable need for a comprehensible and precise explanation as to how Egypt succumbed in the Second Intermediate Period to foreign rule. It is, however, likely to be a false image. The reality is probably more prosaic and certainly less dramatic.

The term Hyksos was first employed (according to the Jewish historian Josephus in his *Contra Apionem*) by the Egyptian historian Manetho, who translated it to mean 'shepherd-kings'. It is thus an inaccurate rendering of the earlier designation of these interlopers by the Egyptians of the time as *hikau khasut* or 'rulers of foreign countries'. As such it was employed by them to refer specifically to the ruling caste of the invaders, whereas the term Hyksos has become synonymous with the whole people.

The rule of the Hyksos can be seen as the climax of waves of Asiatic immigration and infiltration into the north-eastern Delta of the Nile that are known to have occurred from the late 12th Dynasty onwards, and which had become widespread by the 13th Dynasty. Retaining their distinctive cultural identity, these Asiatics began in an opportunistic fashion to insinuate themselves into Egyptian society, and ultimately to assert their own political identity and interests amid the growing weakness and virtual anarchy of the late Middle Kingdom. By 1720 BC they were strong enough to have gained control of the town of Avaris in the north-eastern Delta, the site subsequently becoming the capital of the Hyksos kingdom. Within 50 years Memphis, the ancient northern capital of Egypt, had fallen to them.

Nonetheless, the relative slowness of their advance southwards from the Delta seems to support the argument that the process of takeover was gradual and that it did not turn on the possession of overwhelming military superiority. It seems far more reasonable to infer that the superior military technology of the Hyksos was but an adjunct to their exploitation of the political weakness of the late Middle Kingdom, the collapse of which was finally brought about by their own success. Notwithstanding, the Hyksos, having established themselves in Lower Egypt, eschewed any further expansion southwards—although reducing the rest of Egypt to vassaldom. Their capacity to maintain this hold over the rest of Egypt was undoubtedly a consequence of the effectiveness of their military forces.

Although regarded as the legitimate rulers of the whole country, the Hyksos kings of the 15th Dynasty tolerated rival claimants, the most important of which was the 17th or Theban dynasty of native Egyptians. A formal border defining their respective territories was established, and by the third year of the reign of Kamose—the last pharaoh of the 17th Dynasty—lay at Cusae, near modern Asyut in Middle Egypt. For the Theban dynasts the continued diminution of native Egyptian power was further compounded by the loss of Nubia and its valuable natural and human resources as the rulers of Cush (southern Nubia, extending to the southern end of the second cataract) extended their own power northwards.

Whilst archaeology has revealed a relatively austere culture in Thebes as a consequence, in the period of peace between Hyksos and Thebes trading links allowed the native Egyptians to acquire the benefits of the knowledge and techniques the invaders had brought with them from Palestine and beyond. It was due to the Hyksos that hump-backed Zebu cattle made their appearance in Egypt. New vegetable and fruit crops were cultivated; and the production begun of higher-quality pottery and linen arising from the introduction of an improved potter's wheel and the vertical loom. It was, however, the diffusion of innovations with more obviously military applications, such as bronze-working, which went far to compensate for the technological backwardness of Middle Kingdom Egypt compared to the rest of the Near East. With such expertise the Theban kingdom could begin to exploit and master the production and use of

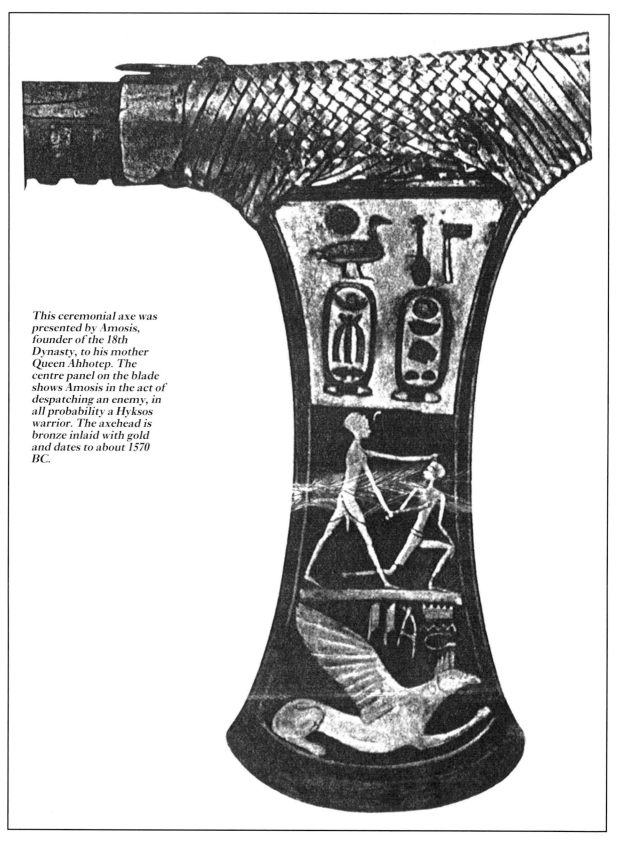

This ceremonial axe was presented by Amosis, founder of the 18th Dynasty, to his mother Queen Ahhotep. The centre panel on the blade shows Amosis in the act of despatching an enemy, in all probability a Hyksos warrior. The axehead is bronze inlaid with gold and dates to about 1570 BC.

bronze weapons, chariots and composite bows —which they had acquired from their foreign overlords, and which were the key to the continued Hyksos domination over them.

More importantly, the baleful experience of foreign rule had done much to shatter a traditional mindset expressed in the Old and Middle Kingdom's presumption of the superiority of Egyptian culture and the security of the state in the face of external threats. The perception that Egypt's boundaries in the east were not inviolable was to result in the formulation of a strategy that was to govern Egyptian military and foreign policy in Nubia and the Levant for the next three hundred years.

## War of Liberation

The beginning of outright Theban resistance to the rule of the Hyksos may date from the reign of Seqenenre Tao II, whose extensively damaged skull strongly points to his death in battle. It is with his son Kamose, however, that the first explicit attempts were made to 'liberate' Egypt when the decision was taken to open hostilities against the Hyksos king, Apophis. It is clear from the stela on which Kamose recorded the details of his campaign that this aggression was directed as much against those Egyptians who had collaborated with the foreigners as it was against the Hyksos themselves: '... I shall burn up their places, made into red mounds forever, because of the damage which they did in this part of Egypt, they who gave themselves over to serving the Asiatics, after they had abandoned Egypt, their mistress.' The sentiments expressed betoken the emergence of a distinctive sense of Egyptian nationalism and a deep feeling of resentment against those who had colluded with the enemy. Indeed, whilst the Hyksos themselves provided the core of their army in the form of élite chariot troops and some infantry, the bulk of their forces were native Egyptians supplied by those Lower Egyptian nomarchs who actively supported them.

*One of the most important contributions of the Hyksos to Egyptian culture was knowledge of bronze-working, enabling the Egyptians to produce thrusting daggers like this one to equip their soldiers. This particular weapon has a bronze blade ribbed for strength. The gold-covered hilt may even suggest that this was the sort of weapon awarded by the pharaohs for bravery as 'the gold of valour.' (British Museum)*

Nubia was a region of great importance in the New Kingdom as a source of gold and other raw materials, and was ruled by an effective Egyptian administration; it was also regarded as a good recruiting ground for auxiliary soldiers. The Medjay, similar in appearance to Nubian prisoners illustrated here and extensively employed as scouts and skirmishers by Kamose, came from this region. (C. el Mahdy)

The campaign Kamose launched in his third year was in the traditional Egyptian fashion of a waterborne attack, supported by tribal mercenary troops from Nubia (who can be identified as the Medjay) operating along the banks. These soldiers had been extensively employed as scouts and light infantry since the late Old Kingdom, and were in the van of the Theban assault on the southernmost Hyksos stronghold at Nefrusy. That Kamose's attack may have come without warning is implied by the lack of any suggestion that the Thebans engaged the main enemy forces in battle. Indeed Kamose's account of the capture of many Hyksos ships loaded with weapons, and the impunity with which he sailed past the walls of their capital of Avaris in the eastern Delta, strongly supports such a view. Contrary to the more

grandiose claims made by the king for this raid, it achieved little except to serve notice of Theban intent to rid Eygpt of the foreigners. It fell not to Kamose, however, but to his younger brother Amosis finally to free Egypt of their domination.

Having first defeated the Egyptian allies of the Hyksos in Middle Egypt, Amosis and the Theban forces took Memphis before beginning the final advance into the eastern Delta in order to lay siege to Avaris. An initial waterborne operation was followed up by a prolonged siege. Our only contemporaneous account of these events is to be found in the biographical record of the captain of a vessel in the service of the king whose namesake he was. His description of events clearly demonstrates the amphibious nature of the Egyptian operations. Ah-mose, son of Eben, tells us that '. . . I was taken on the ship *Northern*, because I was valiant. Thus I used to accompany the Sovereign—(to whom be) life, prosperity, health!—on foot, following his excursions in his chariot'.

We are here presented with one of the first references to the employment of chariots by the Egyptian forces. The inference is, however, that apart from the vehicle carrying the king, the supporting forces operated on foot, and that in these early days the chariot force available to the Thebans was probably quite small in number. Indeed, a slightly earlier reference to the Hyksos chariots on the Kamose stela implies that their capture was greatly prized. Ah-mose continues: '... When the town of Avaris was besieged, then I showed valour on foot in the presence of his majesty. Thereupon I was appointed to the ship *Appearing in Memphis*. Then there was fighting on the water in the canal Pa-Djedku of Avaris.' The fate of the Hyksos capital is described by Ah-mose: '... Avaris was despoiled. Then I carried off spoil from there: one man, three women, a total of four persons. Then his majesty gave them to me for slaves.'

Although Avaris had fallen Amosis did not believe that Egypt was entirely safe. He pursued the retreating Hyksos into southern Palestine, determined to destroy any residual capacity to mount a counter-offensive. The focus of their stand against the Egyptian advance was the fortress of Sharuhen. The strength of the site was such that it took Amosis three years to force the defences and destroy the Hyksos forces bottled up within. Clearly convinced that this victory had eliminated any immediate threat from the east, the army returned to Egypt, and was then marched south and employed in the successful reconquest of Nubia. With the former Middle Kingdom

fortress of Buhen at the northern end of the second cataract reoccupied and rebuilt, the Egyptians rapidly reasserted their rule over the region.

It was in recognition of his achievement in reuniting the two lands that Amosis was honoured by later generations in having established the 18th Dynasty. By his ejection of the Hyksos from Egypt he had elevated the kingdom to become the greatest in the Near East. Inheriting the mantle of the Hyksos, Amosis was now acknowledged as overlord by the states of Palestine and Syria, no doubt encouraged in their declarations by a military demonstration later in his reign that took him as far north as Djahy (Phoenicia). It is very likely that there was a tacit acceptance that all Asia as far as the Euphrates now rightly constituted Egypt's sphere of influence. The projection of military power far beyond Egypt's eastern frontier as the best and most effective method for her defence now became a keystone of her policy in dealing with

*Although illustrating a unit of infantry escorting members of the seaborne trading expedition sent by Hatshepsut to the 'Land of Punt', these are nevertheless representative of the close-combat troops that formed the core of the army, along with the archers, throughout the New Kingdom period. Weapons comprise spear and bronze-headed axe; protection is provided by the short round-topped shield. The soldier to the rear of the officer carries a composite bow in its case.*

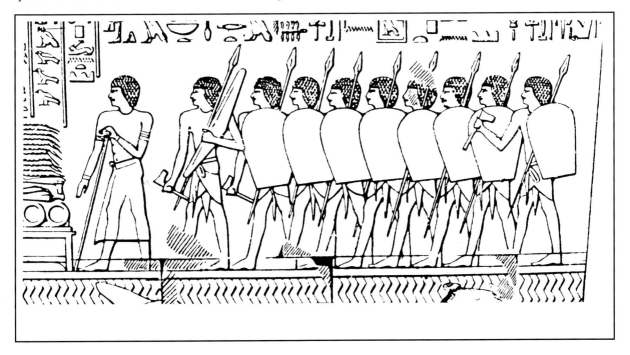

the Levant, and goes far to explain her involvement there over the next four centuries. The corollary of such a policy was the existence of an army suited to the task and a state organised for supporting warfare on a large scale.

In the period of economic reconstruction and political centralisation that followed, the foundations of the Egyptian military state, able to sustain a powerful army and a wide-ranging imperial policy in Palestine and beyond, were laid.

# THE LIMITS OF CONQUEST

Whilst there is little disagreement among scholars that the Egyptian Army was employed in Nubia by Amenophis I, the successor to Amosis, the evidence is ambivalent as to whether he campaigned in Palestine and Syria during his reign. Such that there is suggests

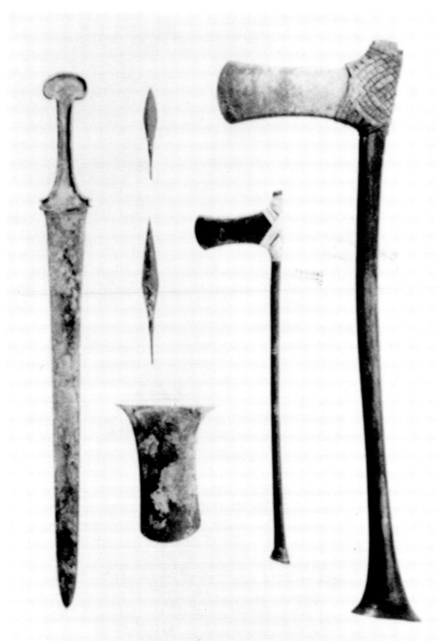

*Shown in greater detail are weapons as carried by the infantry in the previous illustration, typical of the early 18th Dynasty. The primary offensive weapon is the bronze battleaxe. The long dagger (left) is cast in bronze, and represents an intermediate stage before the appearance of the long straight sword introduced to Egypt late in the New Kingdom period by Sherden mercenaries and the 'Sea Peoples'. (C. el Mahdy)*

*Throwsticks were one of the oldest weapons used by the Egyptians. Despite their simplicity their effectiveness meant they were regularly employed by infantry until the end of the New Kingdom. (C. el Mahdy)*

that an Egyptian army may have advanced as far north as the city state of Tunip on the River Orontes. If this did occur, it perhaps indicates Egyptian recognition of the need for a demonstration of strength in the face of the emerging power of the Hurrian Kingdom of Mitanni, whose principal foreign policy objective was to become the control of Syria, a territory regarded by the Egyptians as falling within their own sphere of interest. Indeed, the succession to the throne of Egypt on the death of Amenophis I, in 1625 BC, of a middle-aged and experienced general, suggests an awareness that power and security had become synonymous with the maintenance and employment of her army in defence of her interests. It also implies that the army was already a much more powerful and significant institution in Egyptian society than it ever had been in the earlier Old and Middle Kingdom periods. This was to have a significant impact on internal political developments within Egypt in the centuries ahead.

The years following the accession of Tuthmosis I witnessed a vigorous outburst of military activity as the new pharaoh took the Egyptian army further afield than ever before in its history. Indeed, this pharaoh was to define the limits of territory conquered by Egyptian arms. Although Tuthmosis I did not identify his enemies by name, his employment of the term Naharin, later used by the Egyptians to designate Mitanni, serves to demonstrate that his forces clashed successfully with those of the new power. His placement of a stela, carved into the side of a mountain, on the banks of the Euphrates was a formal means of asserting Egyptian control over all lands to the south of the river. This demonstration of might, some 1,300 kilometres from Egypt, was emulated by his campaign in Nubia. Advancing nearly 800 kilometres to the south of Thebes, Tuthmosis reached Kurgus, upstream of the Fourth Cataract of the Nile.

Significantly, these advances did not result in any permanent occupation of the territory conquered.

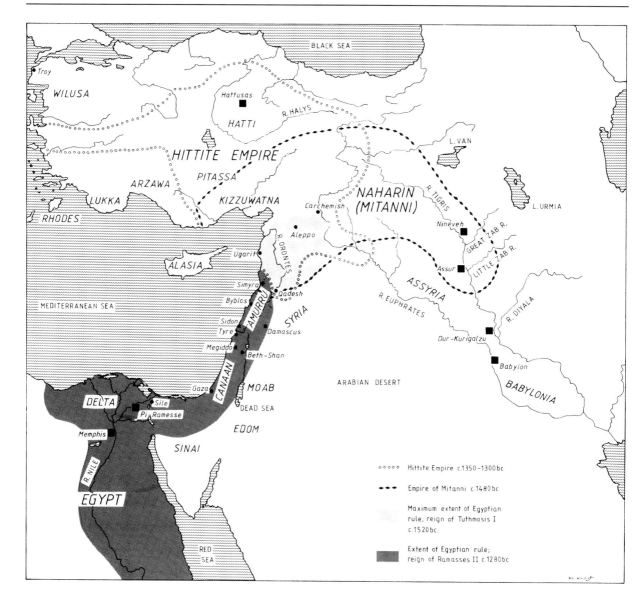

**Legend:**

○○○○○ Hittite Empire c.1350-1300bc

♦♦♦ Empire of Mitanni c.1480bc

Maximum extent of Egyptian rule; reign of Tuthmosis I c.1520bc

Extent of Egyptian rule; reign of Ramasses II c.1280bc

There was no attempt to revise the policy initiated by Amosis whereby the petty states of Syria and Palestine were left free to rule themselves and indulge in their continual internecine warfare as long as they paid their tribute to Egypt. At best these Egyptian expeditions must be seen as pre-emptive raids or reactive responses to perceived threats to Egyptian interests—military demonstrations designed to ensure foreign recognition of those interests, and a forceful reminder to Palestinian and Syrian vassals not to waver from loyalty to their overlord. It had to await the grandson of the first Tuthmosis for Egyptian interests to be secured by a formal imperial policy recognised as 'empire'.

Neither during the reign of Amenophis I or Tuthmosis I was Mitanni strong enough to undermine or destabilise Egyptian authority among its vassals in Syria or Palestine. By the time of Tuthmosis III, however, the military threat from that direction was such that Egypt had little choice but to relinquish her policy of loose hegemony and tread the formal road to empire.

### The Kingdom of Mitanni

The origins of the kingdom of Mitanni lay in the unification of a number of small states in northern Mesopotamia in the second half of the 16th century BC. The heartland of this new kingdom was in the region of the Habur River, where its capital of Washukkani was located, although the exact site has yet to be located. Whilst the population and culture of these petty states and of Mitanni were predominantly Hurrian, the appearance of names of Indo-Aryan origin suggests the domination of the native population by a non-Hurrian chariot-owning military aristocracy. The names of the gods worshipped by this small ruling class were non-Hurrian, and point to a very strong relationship with the Aryan invaders of India. That their power and status was a direct consequence of their military superiority, and that such was vested in their chariots and horses, is indicated by their names. For example, Tushratta, the name of the king of Mitanni who corresponded with Pharaoh Amenophis III, translates as 'owner of terrible chariots', and Biridashwa means 'possessing great horses'. Collectively this chariot-owning aristocracy were called *mariyannu*, a word whose origin is believed to mean 'young warrior.

The contribution of the Mitanni to the history of warfare in the ancient Near East cannot be overstated.

Although they did not introduce the chariot to the region, it was their tactical employment of this weapon in combination with their development of armour for horse and crew that did much to influence not only the armies of Egypt but also those of the Hittites and Assyria. Although bronze scale and lamellar body armour seems to have been a Hurrian invention dating to about the 17th century BC, it was first encountered in quantity being worn by the *mariyannu* of Mitanni. The armour panoply of the noble and royal Mitanni *mariyannu* was very valuable and sophisti-

*Although the Hyksos introduced the composite bow to Egypt, the stave bow did not disappear from the battlefield in the New Kingdom. While the penetrative power of the composite weapon was undeniable it was time-consuming, labour intensive and expensive to produce. Such bows were also sensitive to moisture and could warp unless covered; they were carried in cases by infantry and on the sides of chariots. Stave bows could be produced in large numbers for the bulk of the archers, while the available composite bows went first to the chariotry, where their penetrative power was necessary to pierce mariyannu scale armour. (C. el Mahdy)*

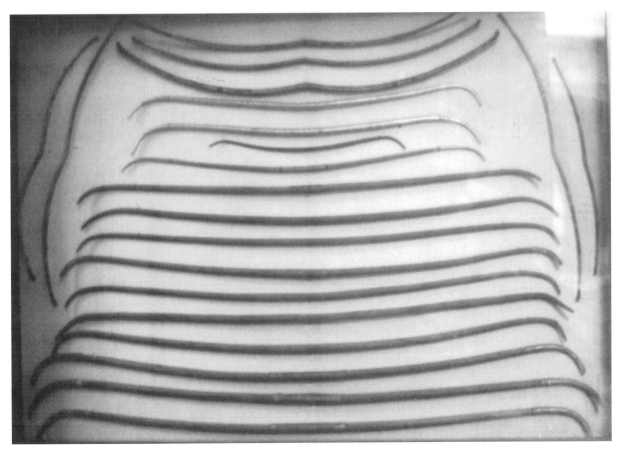

cated in design (see Plate E), and became the measure against which other Near Eastern powers modelled their own; Mitannian influence is clearly discernible in the armour of the Egyptian chariot archer in Plate B. That the Egyptians respected the *mariyannu* and their equipment highly can be gauged by the frequent reference to their capture as booty in the annals of their campaigns in Syria and Palestine. It is also indicated in the way that chariots and associated equipment formed a significant proportion of the dowry sent by King Artatama to Tuthmosis IV when a diplomatic marriage sealed a treaty between Mitanni and Egypt in the early 14th century BC. It is therefore not surprising that the Egyptians viewed with apprehension the rise of this formidable military power

with which they would, before long, be embroiled in inevitable conflict.

Beyond Mitanni, the Hurrian city states of Syria and those ruled by Hurrians and non-Hurrians in Palestine also embraced and emulated the *mariyannu* system and the military technology associated with it. Their military effectiveness goes some way to explain Tuthmosis III needing 17 annual campaigns over a 20-year period in order to control Palestine and Syria.

## The Road to Empire

If during the reigns of Amenophis I and Tuthmosis I Mitanni had yet to make its power strongly felt, Egyptian influence in the Levant showed a marked, albeit self-induced, decline under their two successors, Tuthmosis II and Hatshepsut. During the 20-year reign of Hatshepsut no Egyptian military expedition ventured to the Levant, with the consequence that by the time of her death there was a marked decrease in the tribute received from Egypt's vassals in Syria. In the face of this perceived waning of Egyptian power, Mitanni moved rapidly to assert

*This section of relief shows later New Kingdom close-combat infantry of the time of the Battle of Qadesh. Unlike those illustrated earlier they now wear textile head protection. While a number still carry the bronze battleaxe, others now employ the* khopesh *or 'sickle' sword in addition to the spear and shield. (C. el Mahdy)*

its control over Syria as far as the Mediterranean coast, with most of Egypt's former vassals now acknowledging the king in Washukkani as their overlord.

The real measure of Egyptian weakness, however, can be seen in the manner in which the king of Qadesh on the Orontes had expanded his domain in Syria and then southward into Palestine with total impunity. On news of the death of Hatshepsut in 1482 BC he organised an alliance of city states in Syria and Palestine to challenge Egyptian power in Canaan by seizing the city of Megiddo. We must infer that the King of Qadesh had the tacit, if not open, support of his overlord in Washukkani for this provocation. The city occupied a strategic position astride the main trade route between Egypt and Mesopotamia. Not only did this have economic implications for the kingdom; but the audacity of the act itself promised, unless dealt with quickly, to undermine the credibility of Egypt's rule among her vassals in Canaan. At risk was the whole of her security position in Canaan and the integrity of the eastern borders of Egypt itself.

The foreign policy initiated by Tuthmosis III as a response, and the military campaigns undertaken to realise it, bear all the hallmarks of an underlying grand strategy clearly formulated in advance and designed to address the situation Egypt now found itself in. The policy of leaving vassals to their own devices upon payment of tribute turned on the willingness of the Egyptian pharaohs to undertake regular armed demonstrations in Palestine and Syria. In the absence of such reminders the fickle allegiances of Syrian and Palestinian city states could no longer be assured. Such circumstances now obtained; and also served to demonstrate how different was the situation in the Levant from the time of Amosis, when the policy was originally formulated. Egypt was now opposed by a major power in Mitanni where none had existed before, a power able to challenge her pretensions to suzerainty over the region. Mitanni was determined to undermine Egyptian rule in the Levant by seizing every opportunity to exploit Egyptian weakness.

Tuthmosis III clearly saw that Egypt's situation required a fundamental shift in her strategy. Loose hegemony was no longer appropriate; what was required was a recognisably imperial policy. Palestine and Syria were to be controlled and rebellion pre-

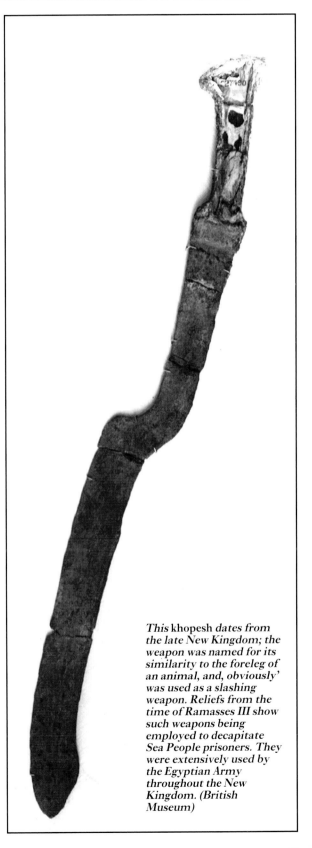

*This khopesh dates from the late New Kingdom; the weapon was named for its similarity to the foreleg of an animal, and, obviously' was used as a slashing weapon. Reliefs from the time of Ramasses III show such weapons being employed to decapitate Sea People prisoners. They were extensively used by the Egyptian Army throughout the New Kingdom. (British Museum)*

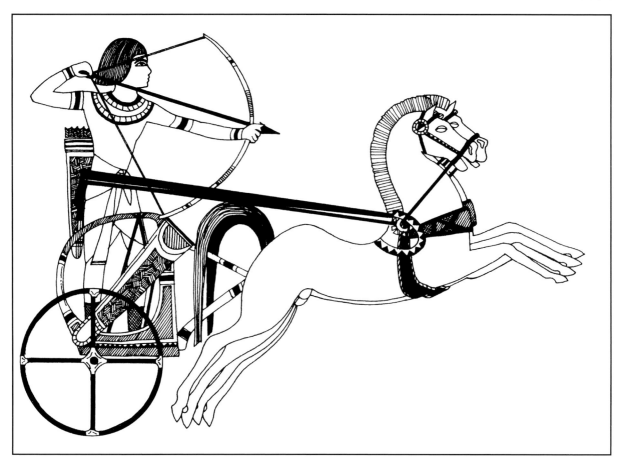

*From the time of the defeat of the Hyksos until the end of the 14th century BC Egyptian chariots strongly resembled those of their Canaanite mentors. Apart from the lightweight design of the body a fundamental distinguishing feature of all chariots prior to the reign of Tuthmosis IV is the four-spoked wheel. Although chariots were built in Egypt, many were given as tribute by Canaanite and Syrian vassals. Here the chariot is being employed for hunting. The driver has wound the reins around his waist, freeing his hands to shoot his bow. (courtesy Firebird books)*

vented by the imposition of military garrisons, and administered by provincial governors under the direct control of the pharaoh. The loyalty of vassal rulers was to be further encouraged by removing their sons to Egypt as hostages.

It is clear, however, that even Tuthmosis III never envisaged the region being totally subjugated and permanently occupied by the army. Such a grandiose model of empire was probably beyond Egypt's resources, and was not the appropriate mechanism to achieve her more limited objectives. In that sense the term 'empire' is used of Egypt's vassal territories in a different way than when utilised, for example, to describe the relationship of Rome to the territories she conquered. At best Egypt's attitude to her vassal territories can be described as indifferent. The military campaigns of Tuthmosis were designed to ensure a more effective control over territories seen to be of value for security reasons and as 'milch cows' from which the maximum economic benefit could be extracted in the form of annual tribute. Inasmuch as Tuthmosis III saw Mitanni as a threat to such a policy he assumed that it was self-evident that it would inevitably lead to a direct clash of arms between the two great powers. It is a measure of his genius that all his campaigns in Palestine and Syria were conscious steps towards ensuring that the inevitable confrontation would be brought about on his terms.

The demise of Hatshepsut allowed Tuthmosis III to exercise sole rule as pharaoh for the first time in his 22-year reign. His response to the challenge of the hostile coalition was typical of the man: measured, but very rapid. In short order he led the Egyptian army into Palestine to do battle with the enemy force. Although inactive for some time, there is no doubting that under the command of this dynamic and remarkable king, who is regarded by many as the greatest pharaoh to have occupied the throne of Egypt, the army was superbly trained, equipped, and well prepared for the contest of arms facing it. Above all, it must be assumed that it was highly motivated, governed as it was by an overwhelming desire to vent its professional frustration on the enemy and redress the effect of the years of self-induced weakness that had brought Egyptian power and prestige beyond its borders to such a sorry pass. It would seem most apposite at this point, with Egypt on the road to empire, to explore very briefly the way the state had evolved to service the needs of the military, and to examine in outline the army itself.

# THE MILITARY STATE

The head of the Egyptian state and commander-in-chief of the armed forces (army and navy) was the pharaoh, who, as supreme warlord, exercised absolute control over the machinery of government and resources of the kingdom, and was thus able to wield unhindered power in the pursuit of his aims. The martial nature of this power is reflected in the inscriptions and pharaonic iconography of the 18th and 19th Dynasties, where the king is depicted in traditional style as sun god but is also portrayed as an incarnation of the war god Montu and the personification of Egypt itself.

Preparation for this role began early, with the heir apparent receiving a distinctly military education at the hands of veterans appointed by the pharaoh. Expertise was acquired in all the arts of war, from the handling of weapons and ships to tactics, strategy and administration. In a society which had acquired a veneration for martial virtues the prowess of the pharaoh in the use of the chariot and bow was highly esteemed. Indeed, it is clear that Tuthmosis III, his son Amenophis II and others were very proud of their skill with these weapons, which was clearly necessary, as in war the pharaoh assumed total control of the army on campaign. Not only did this entail the pharaoh defining the strategy and plan of campaign but also his personal involvement on the field of battle. Tuthmosis III, Amenophis II and Ramasses II were all renowned for their leadership of their chariot corps in battle, and their personal bravery seems never to have been in question.

The concentration of power in the hands of the pharaoh meant that he alone controlled the diverse machinery of government. Clearly such responsibilities demanded men of great self-confidence, intellect, stamina, ability and vision. As in the case of the kings of Assyria, the fortunes of the state were heavily dependent on the quality of whomsoever occupied the throne. It was indeed fortunate for Egypt that during the period of the New Kingdom the throne was occupied by one pharaoh of genius and many of lesser, but nonetheless very high, calibre.

The reorganisation of the state under Amosis saw the emergence of the professional military as a distinct caste in Egyptian society. The maintenance of a standing army able to deploy the full panoply of weapons and resources consistent with late Bronze Age warfare required the creation of new administrative and economic structures within the state. Thus the provision of very large quantities of bronze weapons, such as *khopesh* swords and vast numbers of arrowheads, could only be sustained by a state bureaucracy that oversaw the provision of the raw materials for the metal, and arsenals that produced the weapons themselves. This ranged from the production of shields, chariots and bows in state workshops, to ships for the navy in the dockyard at Memphis. These activities are well attested in a number of paintings from tombs of the New Kingdom period. In addition, no state could support a chariot arm unless it made arrangements for regular horse supply. Whilst it is clear that numbers of horses were captured in battle by the Egyptian army, and given as tribute by vassals in Palestine and Syria, the state provided stud farms and grazing land in order to ensure that the army had all the horses it needed. When consideration is given to the resources necessary to sustain Egypt's standing army, then the phenomenon of war providing the means to sustain war becomes very clear. It provides a significant insight into pharaonic motives for laying hands on Syria and Nubia, both of which were extremely rich in resources.

The structure of the military administration in the early New Kingdom mirrored that of the civil administration. The garrison headquarters of the northern army corps lay at Memphis and that for the south at Thebes, each under the command of a senior officer of the army; later a third was added, and Ramasses II added a fourth. Each was named after the god of the region in which it was based, that in Thebes being named for Amun, in Memphis for Ptah and in Heliopolis, Re. The army formed in the 19th Dynasty and based at Pi-Ramasses was named for Set (Sutekh). The generals in command at these centres were charged with the training of recruits, with their supply to military units and garrisons, and the provision of royal escorts and parade troops. Records of recruitment and stocks of military supplies and the myriad other administrative details lay in the hands of the military scribes, who were under the control of the King's Scribe of Recruits and the Chief Scribes of the Army. They in their turn answered to the pharaoh's vizier, who also oversaw the work of the 'general staff' of the army. This military bureaucracy, imbued with all the scribal traditions of Egyptian administration, maintained a thorough and up-to-date record of the army's strength. It was this administrative efficiency which goes some way to ac-

counting for the status of the army of Egypt in the New Kingdom as one of the most formidable of the Late Bronze Age.

It is a measure of the attraction of the army as a career to the young men of Egypt that denunciations of the military life are frequently to be found in the school writings of New Kingdom scribes. Indeed, as the demands on the army increased so did the opportunities for advancement through its ranks for wealthy and lowly alike. While those of high birth could secure positions in élite units such as the chariot corps, able commoners could achieve promotion to officer status. No better illustration of this can be offered than the career of Horemhab, who

◄ *Although Egypt acquired a chariot arm in the wake of the defeat of the Hyksos, the limited availability of horses prevented its rapid expansion. It was only towards the end of the reign of Tuthmosis III that it reached a large size. Horses were one of the most valued forms of booty from campaigns; another major source of supply was from tribute—in this picture we see two horses being brought to Egypt. Also of significance is the partial image of the child on the shoulder of the figure on the right. From the reign of Tuthmosis III onwards Canaanite and Syrian vassal rulers were required to send their sons to Egypt as hostages for their own good behaviour. These sons were brought up with Egyptian royal children 'to serve their lord and stand at the portal of the king'. (British Museum)*

▶ *Regarded as the greatest pharaoh ever to occupy the throne of Egypt, Tuthmosis III conducted no less than 17 campaigns in Canaan and Syria to assert his domination of the Levant. His Megiddo campaign demonstrates qualities that make it understandable why he is sometimes referred to as the 'Napoleon of Ancient Egypt'. (C. el Mahdy)* began his army career as a scribe and ended up as pharaoh. Other pharaohs who began their careers in the army included Ay, Ramasses I and, as we have already seen, Tuthmosis I. Bravery was very frequently rewarded by the 'valour of gold,' which was awarded in the form of gold ornaments and weapons. (Ah-mose speaks of being given it twice by Amosis)

Land grants, slaves, and a share in the booty of campaign provided many an incentive for voluntary enlistment. The caste nature of the Egyptian standing military was reinforced by the tendency for military service to become hereditary as son followed father into the ranks. This was fostered and encouraged by the practice of establishing military colonies throughout Egypt. However, alongside the regular army served those called up by conscription, their names being drawn from the district registers kept by the Scribe of Recruits. The Middle Kingdom draft ratio of one in every hundred eligible had increased substantially towards the close of the New Kingdom period, so that in the reign of Ramasses III one in every ten men eligible for conscription was 'called to the colours'. It is clear from a number of contemporary accounts that in some cases the conscription was more like impressment, with bodies of armed troops present to enforce the call-up and separate the chosen men from their families. This is not surprising; by the time of Ramasses III the large number of men being conscripted into the army was itself symptomatic of the military dangers facing Egypt on her very borders.

*The basis of the military power of the Canaanite city states was the élite chariotry known as mariyannu. This example, taken from the reliefs on the chariot body of* *Tuthmosis IV, shows the essential features and appearance of these Canaanite vehicles and their crews. (Firebird Books)*

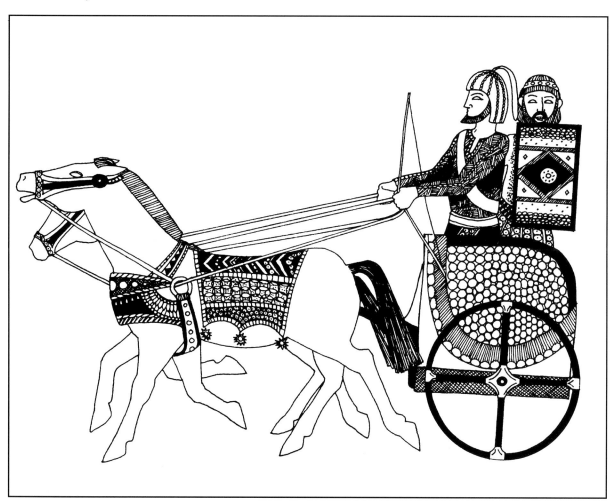

# THE NEW KINGDOM ARMY AT WAR

The army that Tuthmosis III led out beyond the frontier fortress of Sile to do battle with the enemy coalition at Megiddo in 1482 BC differed little from that taken further northward by Ramasses II to confront the Hittites at Qadesh one hundred and eighty years later. While the army of Ramasses was certainly larger, deploying four field armies rather than two, and while the appearance of soldiers changed somewhat to take account of technical developments and the lessons of combat, there was in all other respects a remarkable continuity.

Notwithstanding the introduction of the chariot, the Egyptian standing army of the New Kingdom was, like its Middle Kingdom predecessor, mainly an infantry force. In this the Egyptian army differed from those of Mitanni or the Syrian and Canaanite city states, whose primary arm was the chariotry. This reflects what were undoubtedly two very strong advantages the Egyptian army could exploit. Relative to her opponents Egypt's large population allowed the deployment of a large infantry force; and the experience of centuries in the organisation and discipline of large bodies of men translated themselves naturally to the army.

## The infantry

The infantry were of two sorts. The archers, equipped either with the older stave or newer composite bows, would be deployed in linear formation but employed according to the nature of the opposition. When faced by lightly protected troops such as the Libyans, massed volleys alone were frequently sufficient to effect the necessary level of destruction. Against more heavily armed and protected infantry the archers would be employed to deliver heavy covering fire for the close combat infantry, known as *nakhtu-aa* or 'the strong-arm boys'. These would advance rapidly, discharging their spears in the process before closing with an enemy already softened up by the supporting fire of the archers, and setting to with their bronze *khopesh* swords or long mace axes. While

there was clear co-operation between these two branches of the infantry, there is no extant evidence to suggest they operated together in close combat formations. Infantry of either sort were normally deployed in company units of approximately 200 to 250 men, distinguishable on the field of battle by the company standard; the morale and status of each company was enhanced by titles closely related to the images on the standard. Examples include that of a Nubian company under Amenophis II called 'Bull in Nubia', and others under Amenophis III called 'Manifest in Justice' and 'Splendour of Aten'. Movement control was effected by signals from war trumpets, examples of which have been recovered from tombs.

## The chariot arm

It is clear that given the central role of the infantry in the Egyptian army it would become a primary target for the mass chariotry of the Syrians and Canaanites. Ideally they would attempt to surprise the Egyptian infantry when vulnerably strung out on the march. Indeed, it was in order to deny them exactly that opportunity that Tuthmosis III chose to avoid the obvious line of march, through either the northern or southern entry points into the Vale of Esdraelon, on his approach to Megiddo. However, such a tactic was used very successfully by the Hittites at Qadesh when their massed chariots crashed into the army corps of Re. Egyptian infantry, while able to deploy to receive chariots, depended mainly on their own chariot units to defend them from the enemy's. It can be seen how very different was the Egyptian use of the chariot arm from that of the *mariyannu*. A primary role was the support and protection of the infantry, by denying enemy chariotry the opportunity of surprising them on the march or of allowing them to harry the infantry from a distance and reduce their numbers through attrition by long-range archery.

The Hyksos had been the great mentors for the Egyptians in chariot warfare, and while the latter drew quite freely on the technology of the Canaanites and others in the development of their own chariot arm it is apparent that from early on it developed in a distinctively idiosyncratic fashion. This was reflected in the design of their chariots. Compared to those of the Hittites, Mitanni, and the *mariyannu* of Syria and Canaan they appear quite delicate, even effete for

warfare. This impression was clearly more apparent than real. A heavy chariot is designed for the charge and close-order combat; the weight of the machine is itself part of its offensive potential, and presupposes the availability of open terrain to allow acceleration and momentum to build up during the charge. Such vehicles would be totally inappropriate either for the primary tasks required of Egyptian chariotry or for the terrain of Egypt or Canaan. While Egyptian chariot units were employed in scouting ahead of the advancing army they could not always ensure that enemy units in hiding would be discovered; thus reaction time when attacked was crucial. If supporting chariots were to protect the infantry rapid acceleration to meet the charging enemy was vital. Lightweight chariots such as those used by the Egyptians could fulfil such a role. The lightweight but very sturdy design also reflects the nature of the terrain over which they were normally employed. Deserts and uplands are not at all suitable for heavy chariots (as the Assyrians discovered), and as the Egyptians both traversed and fought over such terrain in Egypt, Sinai and Canaan, the chariot needed to be suited for the task.

It is clear that tactics to meet their heavy brethren

in their opponents' armies were well developed and successfully employed by Egyptian chariot units. They were above all designed to exploit the inherent speed and manoeuvrability of the Egyptian machines. Contact with the heavier armed and armoured chariots of the Mitanni and Hittites did at least see the emergence of six-spoked wheels to accommodate the weight of the more heavily protected crews that we find depicted in late 18th- and 19th-Dynasty paintings. Even so, the essential virtues of the Eygptian vehicles were preserved.

The Egyptian chariots would charge the enemy chariots in well-spaced line abreast. Distance between each machine was quite deliberate, to allow a rapid wheel and turn once the enemy line had been penetrated, and to prevent too close a passage through the line by the enemy. The intention was to use archery at longer range and javelins at short range to cause as much havoc as possible. If the ferocity of the attack caused the enemy to break off, then the rapidly pursuing Egyptians could inflict heavy casualties.

Essential to the effectiveness of the chariots were the lightly armed chariot runners. These troops, equipped with bow and javelin, fulfilled a number of functions. Following the charge they would capture or despatch enemy crewmen, and where possible rescue those of their own who had crashed. Most im-

*In the wake of his father's death Amenophis II embarked upon a number of campaigns to suppress rebellion in Canaan and Syria. A man of great physical strength, he was renowned for his skill with the composite bow. A relief at Karnak shows his ability to shoot his bow from a moving chariot and penetrate copper ingots used as targets. (C. el Mahdy)*

portantly, they were to be prepared to receive opposing chariots as they penetrated the Egyptian line and to deal with as many as possible before they could wheel and return. The much more rapid turn of the Egyptian vehicles meant that the enemy could be caught between chariots and runners.

### Auxiliary troops

As with all other imperial powers of the ancient world, the Egyptians employed large numbers of auxiliary troops. We have already referred to the Medjay, who were used extensively under the early New Kingdom. Other foreign troops included those who served to fulfil their vassal obligations, and these would have included contingents from the city states of Syria and Canaan. Others arrived in the Egyptian army by a more circuitous route, having started out as prisoners of war, whose obvious fighting potential led to their being incorporated into the army. These included Nubians, Libyans and the famous Sherden, one contingent of which was employed as an élite guard infantry unit by Ramasses II.

### The field armies

On campaign, the army corps mentioned above would act as self-contained field armies embracing all arms. An advance into enemy territory would see these field armies separated by some 10km but within supporting distance of each other, communications being maintained by riders or chariots. The logic of this organisation is apparent given that the principal tactic of the opposition was the employment of skirmishing chariotry to strike at an advancing army on the march. The short distance between each corps ensured that in the event of the protecting chariots of one being swept away, support could be moved forward quickly to help the infantry now under attack. This, however, did not always work, as at Qadesh (see diagrams).

The armies could either be employed in concert to form a single body for battle; or separated, where need demanded, to address individual tasks, with orders for later reassembly. The self-contained nature of their organisation is clearly indicated in a description of a campaign undertaken by Seti I in northern Palestine in about 1318 BC: '. . . Thereupon his majesty sent the first army of Amun, "Mighty of Bows", to the town of Hamath; the first army of Re, "Plentiful of Valour", to the town of Beth-Shan; and the first army of Seth, named "Strong of Bows" to the town of Yanoam'.

Although many pharaohs boasted of their prowess in forming the army into a battle line and took great care with their dispositions, the Egyptians adopted the conventional deployment of the infantry in the centre with the chariots on the flanks. It was rare for the Egyptians to act in a defensive fashion on the battlefield unless, as at Qadesh, they did not possess the initiative and had the battle forced upon them.

It is clear that they possessed the means to conduct siege warfare. On the advance toward Megiddo Tuthmosis III detached troops under the command of his general Djehuty to lay siege to the city of Jaffa; Amosis laid siege to Sharuhen for three years, and Tuthmosis III to Megiddo for seven months. When sieges are illustrated in the annals, as in Merneptah's campaign in Palestine, the principal method of assault is shown as being by scaling ladders, and by infantry attempting to break into the city by using axes on the wooden gates. With the large number of fortified cities throughout Palestine and Canaan it is understandable that the Egyptians saw the battlefield as the means of forcing a military decision and, like other powers such as the Assyrians, they tried to avoid sieges where possible.

### The navy

The use of river vessels and ships in Egyptian warfare is as old as conflict in Egypt itself. In the New Kingdom the 'navy' was not seen as a separate service but as an integral part of the army and was employed extensively in amphibious operations. We have already mentioned such operations being conducted by Kamose and Amosis in the war against the Hyksos. Tuthmosis III had a large fleet built at the royal dockyard at Perunefer, near Memphis, these vessels being employed to transport elements of the army along the coast to ports in the Lebanon on a number of occasions in support of his operations against the city states of southern Syria and Mitanni itself. Many of these ships were adapted cargo vessels.

The best illustrations of Egyptian warships in action are to be found on the walls of the temple at Medinet Habu, which detail the defeat of a fleet of vessels belonging to the 'Sea Peoples' during the reign of Ramasses III. The crews of such vessels were infantry companies designated to train and then serve on ships, although those vessels depicted on the Medinet Habu reliefs carried a crew of about fifty. The whole crew were trained as marines and, although essentially fighting men, doubled up as the oarsmen and general shiphandlers.

In combat some 20 of the crew would be delegated to row the vessel while the remainder formed the combat troops for the encounter. Pulling directly towards the enemy vessels, the marines would use bows and slings to rake the decks while a number of the crew would throw grappling hooks into the rigging with the object of either capsizing or boarding the enemy ship. If the latter, then as the vessels closed a number of marines carrying spears for close-order thrusting would board the enemy vessel under cover of archery from their own ship. It is a scene from this battle that has been illustrated in Plate J. The defeat

*In the reign of Tuthmosis IV Egyptian chariots began to throw off their Canaanite character and assume a more native style. By the end of his reign the Egyptian chariot wheel had assumed its standard six-spoked form. This example was recovered from the tomb of Yuya, the father-in-law of Amenophis III. (C. el Mahdy)*

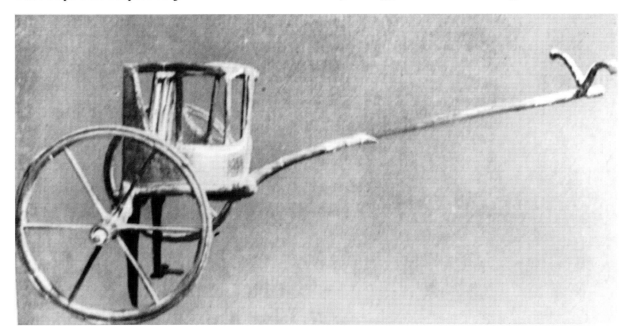

of the Sea Peoples at the mouth of the Nile was a consequence of a carefully laid trap in which the Egyptians herded the enemy vessels towards the shore, where ranks of archers poured arrows onto their decks. Many of the Sea Peoples' vessels were capsized; large numbers of prisoners were taken, and many others drowned, such details being carefully rendered in the Medinet Habu reliefs.

# THE BATTLE OF MEGIDDO

It was not only Napoleon who made war with his soldiers' legs. Within nine days of leaving Egypt Tuthmosis III and his army had reached Gaza in southern Canaan. The march through Sinai by the road known as the 'Ways of Horus' suggests a marching rate of about 15 miles per day; however, the rate of march slowed to about eight per day thereafter, perhaps indicative of fatigue, or of care being exercised as the advance reached territory regarded as potentially or actually hostile. The need to detach units under the redoubtable general Djehuty to place Jaffa under

siege points to wide support for the coalition in southern Canaan. It is also significant that Tuthmosis felt it necessary to besiege to a city that lay astride his communications and possible line of retreat.

### The approach

Arriving in the vicinity of Megiddo by mid-May, Tuthmosis called a council of his senior staff officers to discuss the options available to the army. Critical study of the text describing the conference and the battle (carved on the walls of the Temple of Karnak) suggests that it is very much a device for projecting the king in a heroic role. Notwithstanding, the subject matter of their deliberations was the choice of route into the Plain of Esdraelon, where Megiddo was sited. Of the three, two offered less difficult approaches. The third, the Aruna 'road', was through a narrow and difficult pass over the ridge that was presumed (certainly by the enemy coalition) to be too difficult for an army to use. Its principal advantage lay in its

*Here two other examples of late 18th-Dynasty chariots, also recovered from tombs, are shown on display in the Cairo Museum. Prominent on both is the large grab-rail extending forward from the top of the cab, which was employed to steady the archer when the chariot advanced at speed. (C. el Mahdy)*

direct approach to Megiddo itself, for it would allow the army to debouch onto the Plain of Esdraelon less than a mile from the city. The sentiments about the third route were, according to the report, unanimous among the pharaoh's generals: they believed that the dangers outweighed the advantages. To go by this way meant that 'horse must follow horse, and man after man'; to be caught when strung out in such a manner was a recipe for disaster.

The discussion of the options could not, however, have taken place purely on the level of abstractions. Tuthmosis and his generals must have known, through reconnaissance, that the coalition forces, particularly their chariotry, were deployed to cover the approaches of the two easier routes to Megiddo, in particular the one from Taanach. They would have been ideally placed to attack the Egyptian forces as they entered the plain. The army corps would have been surprised while on the march, separated, and vulnerable to the mass chariot attacks of the *mariyannu*, whose intentions were not only to inflict a sound defeat on the Egyptian chariot units, but—once the latter's effectiveness had been severely impaired—to begin a process of attrition of the infan-

try by long-range archery. Thus, even before the Egyptian army was finally able to deploy for battle, the enemy could have inflicted very heavy losses. Canaanite tactics were well known to the Egyptians, and not withstanding the 20-year hiatus in operations in the region there must have been plenty of officers present who had personal experience of fighting the *mariyannu* in Canaan.

Tuthmosis clearly believed that the benefits of the more difficult route far outweighed the disadvantages, and was perhaps confirmed in the correctness of his own view by the vehemence with which his own generals argued their corner. If they were prepared to risk the losses entailed in approaching Megiddo via one of the other two routes rather than take the Aruna road, how much more likely was it that the enemy, thinking in the same way, would have left the more difficult route undefended? By the time the enemy

*This graphic gives an excellent profile view of a chariot of the Amarna Age. Clearly shown is the six-spoked wheel and the case for the composite bow. The placement of the axle at the extreme rear of the cab gave the vehicle a remarkable turning facility, a factor of great importance in Egyptian chariot tactics. (Firebird Books)*

*Under Pharaoh Amenophis III Egypt reached its apogee of wealth and power. Abroad she was at peace with Mitanni; the lands of her 'empire' were quiescent. (C. el Mahdy)*

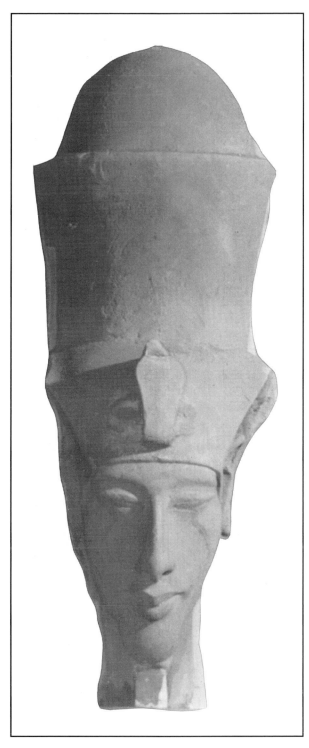

*It was in the reign and aftermath of his successor Amenophis IV (Akhenaten) that Egypt's concerns turned inwards as it was convulsed by religious revolution and political reaction. It was during this period that the Hittites destroyed the power of Mitanni and emerged as the dominant power in the Levant. (C. el Mahdy)*

had discovered his error the Egyptians would have gained the benefit of surprise and the army would be deployed on the plain, ready for battle and having entailed none of the losses attendant on using the other routes. Notwithstanding the continued doubts of his officers, Tuthmosis announced his decision in a manner that gives some insight into his grasp of psychology: '... My majesty shall proceed upon this Aruna road! Let him of you who wishes come in the following of my majesty! Whatever their doubts about his plan, their loyalty to their lord, as he very well knew, was not in doubt!'

Over the following two days the army ascended the hills that led to the Aruna road, but it was only in the early hours of the third day that the actual passage through the pass began. At its widest the pass is but 30 feet wide. It is interesting that a number of commentators, in remarking how difficult the route was for chariots, seem to have forgotten that one of the major virtues of the Egyptian design was its lightness: it is certainly more than conceivable that many were carried and the horses led through separately. The passage of the whole army took some 12 hours, and it was not until late in the evening that it was encamped on the plain. Even as the Egyptian army poured out from the pass the leading elements could see the main enemy forces rushing back to cover the approaches to Megiddo, so that by the time night fell the coalition army lay in front of the Egyptian lines and in front of the city. The pharaoh's gamble had paid off, and tactical surprise had been achieved.

That the Egyptian camp was on edge throughout the hours of darkness is clearly implied by the text. The possibility of a night attack could not be discounted, and the pharaoh demanded of the sentries that they '... be steadfast, be steadfast! Be vigilant, be vigilant!' His orders that all the troops prepare themselves and '... make your weapons ready, since one (the pharaoh) will engage in combat with the wretched enemy in the morning' suggests that many had a sleepless night. While the inference is that the pharaoh was optimistic about the outcome, such positive feelings may not have been shared by all. Should the battle be lost then retreat would be extremely difficult, with the rear of the Egyptian army butting up against the hills. The sense of a gamble, a decisive encounter in which a very great deal turned on the outcome, is lost amid the triumphalist language employed in the narrative. As far as we know it was the first major battle in which Tuthmosis was in overall command—and of an army that had not fought a major engagement for some 20 years.

## The deployment

The following morning the pharaoh ordered the deployment of his army. Resplendent in his war chariot of fine gold and electrum, and wearing the 'blue' or war crown, he is described as being 'adorned with the accoutrements of combat, like Horus, the Mighty of Arm, a lord of action like Montu, the Theban, while his father Amun made strong his arms.' The enigmatic phrase 'Now a charge was laid upon the entire army to pass by....' clearly refers to this

deployment, but carries with it the implication that in the movement to their positions the army paraded past the pharaoh. It is not inconceivable that this took place. The spectacle of the Egyptian army, resplendent in full uniform with armour glittering, horse plumes and flags fluttering in the breeze, standards carried aloft, with war trumpets sounding, drums beating, and thunderous shouts of acclaim as they passed the pharaoh's chariot, may well have had a dire impact on the morale of the enemy, who were themselves deploying to their positions for battle. Not the least reason for Tuthmosis ordering such a parade would have been the impact of the spectacle on the Egyptians themselves, many of whom would be seeing combat for the first time: theatre has its part to play in war, and if such a parade did precede the battle then it may well have played a real part in its outcome.

Tuthmosis divided his army into three divisions. The northern wing was anchored in position to the north-west of Megiddo. The pharaoh commanded the centre; and the southern wing was located on a hill to the south of 'the brook of Qina'. The enemy forces

*A number of features in this line drawing from a relief in a tomb at Tell-el-Amarna are of interest. The first four figures on the right of the upper register are foreign soldiers in Egyptian service. The remainder in the row carry standards, which allowed rapid identification of companies on the battlefield. The lower register depicts close-combat infantry. (C. el Mahdy)*

were described as vast, numbering no fewer than 330 kings, each with his own army: 'millions of men, and hundreds of thousands of the chiefest of all the lands, standing in their chariots.'

## The battle

Details of the actual battle are sparse, but the overwhelming impression is that shortly after it began, with a forceful charge by the pharaoh with his chariots from the centre, the enemy line simply folded up under the advance of the Egyptian forces. A wave of panic swept through the coalition army, with weapons, equipment, chariots and horses being abandoned as headlong flight turned into rout. The safety of the walled city was denied, as the inhabitants of Megiddo closed its great gates to stop the Egyptians entering. There then followed the ludicrous sight of knotted sheets being lowered so that at least the high and mighty among the defeated, including the king of Kadesh and the ruler of Megiddo, could be rescued by scrambling up the walls. Many others owed their salvation to the attractions of the vast quantities of booty they had abandoned: '. . . if only his majesty's army had not given their hearts to capturing the possessions of the enemy, they would have captured Megiddo at this time. . . .' It is clear that the official narrative recognised that this breakdown of discipline had robbed the pharaoh of total victory, as Megiddo could have been stormed and taken in the resultant panic. Some have seen in this breakdown of discipline evidence of the poor discipline of the Egyptian army. This is not a self-evident conclusion: there are too many other examples throughout history of well-disciplined and professional armies succumbing to like temptation—Wellington's men at Vitoria in 1813 spring at once to mind.

Tuthmosis placed the city under siege and ordered that it be taken at all costs, '. . . for the ruler of every northern country is in Megiddo, and its capture is the capture of a thousand cities'. A moat was dug around the city and beyond this a wooden palisade was constructed to seal in the populace. It was not until some seven months later, in December 1482 BC, that the city surrendered. The booty listed was vast, but pride of place was given to the 2,041 horses that were taken and used to swell the breeding stock in Egypt.

The victory of Megiddo was of great importance. Its impact was certainly sufficient to render the whole

*The mummified features of Seti I, the second pharaoh of the 19th Dynasty, who made it a basic concern of his foreign policy to confront Hittite power and raise Egypt's standing to pre-eminence in the Near East. (C. el Mahdy)*

of Canaan quiescent for virtually the rest of the reign. The major business of Tuthmosis' campaigns in the next 20 years, however, lay in his contest with Mitanni for the control of Syria.

## The Campaign of Year Thirty-Three

If Megiddo was one of the three most important battles fought by the Egyptian army in the New Kingdom period, one of the most interesting, and most personally satisfying for Tuthmosis III, was the campaign of the thirty-third year of his reign (1471 BC). Immense energies and labours had been expended to prepare the Egyptian army, now battle-hardened, to at last contest with '. . . that wretched Mitannian foe' in the land of Mitanni itself.

The previous years had seen the Egyptian army engaged in a systematic reduction of the power of the city states of the central Syrian coast and hinterland as a necessary prelude to the assault on Mitanni. Although neither Tunip nor Qadesh succumbed to the Egyptian assaults, their power was sufficiently reduced for Tuthmosis to receive rich tribute from other city states formerly under their sway.

In the late spring of 1471 BC large numbers of troops were brought by sea to Syria, disembarking at various ports. These joined up with the bulk of the army, which had marched northwards from Egypt. Using timber from the forests around Byblos, pontoons were constructed to allow the army to make passage across the fast-flowing Euphrates. Having crossed the River Orontes, Tuthmosis and his army had their first successful engagement with troops of Mitanni to the west of the city of Aleppo. Carchemish was the objective, and it was here that the Euphrates was bridged, using the pontoons that had been so laboriously transported northward on ox wagons. It was also here that the pharaoh realised a long-held ambition to emulate his grandfather, and placed his own stela alongside that of the first Tuthmosis. Marching southward along the banks of the river the Egyptians reached as far as Emar before crossing back over it. The booty they had taken was very poor, and the failure to draw Mitanni into a major battle suggests that the king in Washukkani saw this Egyptian foray as nothing more than a raid in strength, with little or nothing but prestige to be gained.

Mitanni never obliged Tuthmosis III with the great battle he would so dearly have loved to fight. Other campaigns in later years would continue to ensure Egyptian control over the region; but the reality of the last 12 years of his reign, when old age prevented him taking the field and the tribute from the region ceased to flow, was that Egyptian control so far north was ephemeral. It was simply too far away from the home base to allow permanent control to be ensured. By the end of his reign, it was clear that Mitanni was once more encroaching upon the region, negating the immense efforts expended by this lion-hearted pharaoh in attempting to bring the region permanently under the sway of Egypt.

## Rapprochement with Mitanni

It was a truism of Egypt's relations with the rulers of its vassal states in the Levant that each owed their allegiance to a particular pharaoh who had earned their respect, and not to Egypt itself. So it was that Amenophis II set out on the road to Syria to suppress the revolt that had broken out there following the death of his father in 1450 BC, and to impose his own stamp on the region. Two campaigns, in the third and seventh years of his reign, saw his armies operating in the vicinity of Qadesh on the Orontes. The first of these was memorable for the ruthless manner in which the rebellion was suppressed, with Amenophis himself executing the ringleaders; six of their bodies were exposed at Thebes, while the seventh was hung to rot on the walls of Napata in Nubia as a grim warning to other potential rebels. His last military foray was to suppress a rebellion in Canaan.

Notwithstanding the official histories of the reigns of Amenophis II and his son Tuthmosis IV, it would seem that Egypt was slowly losing ground to Mitanni in Syria. It was the temporary re-emergence on the scene in northern Syria of the Hittites and the collective threat to Egyptian and Mitannian interests in the region that provided the catalyst for the rapprochement between the two great powers. Tuthmosis IV would seem, however, to have been the principal suitor. The peace treaty was sealed by diplomatic marriages; and by the reign of Amenophis III it is possible to identify a loose status quo and accepted spheres of influence defining Mitanni and Egyptian interests in central Syria, although the power of the latter in this region was slowly waning.

The reign of Amenophis III saw the high point in the wealth, culture and prestige of New Kingdom Egypt. The peace with Mitanni and the quiescence of the Canaanite vassals lent an air of permanency to the international situation. The Amarna tablets, which date from the reign of Amenophis III and his son Amenophis IV (Akhenaten), not only include samples of diplomatic letters but give a unique insight into Canaan in this period. The squabbles between the rulers of the petty states of the region are set alongside accounts of difficulties in controlling the nomadic Sutu and the landless Hapiru. One of the tablets among the Amarna letters bears the name of Suppiluliumas, king of the Hittites, in which he expresses his hopes that the amicable relations estab-

Early New Kingdom Infantry
1: Archer
2: *Nakhtu-aa* close-combat infantry
3: Medjay

A

Early New Kingdom chariot and crew, c1430 BC
1: *Seneny* archer
2: *Kedjen* driver
3: Canaanite peasant levy

B

Mitannian *marjannu* chariot
1: Archer
2: Driver

1&2: Egyptian infantry
3&4: Canaanite *mariyannu*

D

1: Trumpeter
2: Drummer
3-6: Standards (see text commentary for details)

E

1&2: Egyptian close-combat infantry
3&4: Libyan tribal warriors

F

1

3

Late New Kingdom chariot
1: Driver
2: Archer
3: Chariot runner

G

Late New Kingdom archers and mounted messenger
1&2: Archers
3: Mounted messenger

H

Enemies of Egypt: the Hittites
1: Driver
2: Shield bearer
3: Armoured spearman

The naval battle with the Sea Peoples, c1190 BC
(see text commentary for detailed caption)

The Sea Peoples' land invasion
(see text commentary for detailed caption)

K

lished between the land of Hatti and Egypt 'in the reign of the pharaoh's father' can be maintained. It was this man more than any other who dominated the 14th century BC. By his great military campaigns in Syria he recast the map of the ancient Near East, drawing forth from Egypt her last and greatest military effort to secure her imperial interests in the Levant.

# THE HITTITE THREAT

Even as the peoples of the Near East witnessed the revival and expansion of the Hittite realm, it was paralleled by the demise of the Kingdom of Mitanni. The latter power, wracked by internal power struggles, was unable either to resist the military assaults of Suppiluliumas and his army or to withstand the expansion of the Assyrians into their eastern territories. The collapse of Mitanni saw the Hittites take control of all of the former western part of her empire. Although the Egyptians were the nominal allies of Mitanni, their own internal troubles precluded any interference in the events determining the future of Syria.

During the period when Suppiluliumas was redrawing the map of northern Syria, Egypt was preoccupied by the religious reforms of Akhenaten and the reactions to them following his death. Little attention seems to have been paid to Syria, although this is not the same as saying that there was indifference; there was a strong concern that Egypt retain control over the territory between Byblos and Ugarit for trading purposes. However, the means to challenge Hittite power at this time were severely curtailed by major economic problems that precluded any expenditure on military campaigns. The political, religious and economic ferment in the wake of the reign of Akhenaten saw a preoccupation with internal affairs that lasted some 40 years. Even so, pockets of stability in Canaan, where certain cities remained loyal to Egypt while many others were throwing off their allegiance, bely the view that all was chaos beyond the borders of the kingdom.

In the wake of the sack of Washukanni the Hittites pushed further into central Syria. In the same manner

as Mitanni before them, they encouraged their new vassals to foster dissension amongst those states still loyal to Egypt. Nevertheless, the same rationale that had led to Egyptians contesting with Mitanni over Syria still obtained; all that had changed was the name of the threat. As Egypt still claimed suzerainty over the Levant it was merely a matter of time before an Egyptian army tramped northwards once more. It was not until the accession of Seti I in 1318 BC that a determined attempt was made by the Egyptians to recover their position and prestige in Canaan and the Levant.

### The campaigns of Seti I

This new king, the second of the 19th Dynasty, clearly signalled his ambition to restore Egypt's prestige as a great power in the adoption of the title 'Repeater of Birth' for his Horus name. In the four campaigns he fought, of which three were in Canaan and Syria, he laid the foundations for the great contest of arms between his son Ramasses II and the Hittites at Qadesh some 18 years later. However, his battle with the Libyans in Year Three of his reign was but the prelude to increasingly major problems that were to afflict Egypt's western borders at different times throughout the 19th Dynasty.

Exploiting the opportunity provided by reports of a nomadic incursion into the northern Sinai and conflict between a number of cities in eastern Canaan, Seti took his army eastwards across the border in the first year of his reign. However, his movements after dealing with these fairly minor military problems suggest that they were never anything more than a guise to cover an assault on a number of cities in the Lebanon. It would seem that this was envisaged by Seti as the first stage in a longer-term strategy, for in Year Two fragmentary evidence suggests that the Egyptian army moved further north into its old stamping grounds of Syria and assaulted the city of Qadesh. This was clearly seen by the Hittites as a provocation. It was in all probability Seti's intention to initiate hostilities with the northern power in Year Three, had not more pressing matters drawn his attention to Egypt's western border with the eruption of a major incursion by Libyan tribes into the kingdom. The Egyptian victory was sufficient to prevent a repeat attempt until the reign of Ramasses II.

In Year Four occurred the major clash with the

Hittites. Although details are sketchy, it would seem that a major battle took place to the north of Qadesh in which the Egyptians claimed a great victory. Many Hittites were said to have been killed and Seti returned to Egypt with much booty and many captives.

In common with many accounts of Egyptian operations in Syria during the time of Mitanni, it is the inference we can draw from the silence that is important when considering Egypt's relations with the Hittites in the region. Notwithstanding Seti's claims to have inflicted a major defeat on the Hittites and captured Qadesh, the fact that he entered into a treaty with Muwatallish implies that the Egyptian position in central Syria was at best tenuous. It would seem that the treaty recognised both Hittite and Egyptian spheres of influence in the region, but did not demarcate clear and formal boundaries. Nevertheless, Qadesh must have been given up to the Hittites—otherwise we have no way of accounting for the climactic battle for the city fought in the reign of his son and successor, Ramasses II.

# THE BATTLE OF QADESH

Ramasses II was about 25 years of age when he ascended the throne of Egypt in 1304 BC, absolute master of one of the world's great powers. He was young, vigorous, able and resourceful; but above all, full of ambition to emulate his illustrious forebears of the early 18th Dynasty by extending Egypt's northern frontiers to encompass again the territories of central Syria, notwithstanding that those territories lay firmly within the Hittite sphere and that such was tacitly recognised by the treaty agreed with Hatti by his father Seti I. Fulfilment of his ambition meant that Ramasses accepted the inevitability of war with Egypt's powerful northern rival. Although he was unable to engage in military operations in Syria until Year Four of his reign, it is apparent that from an early date much energy was expended within Egypt in preparing the army for its coming contest with Hatti. This included adding a fourth field army to the

order of battle, and the expansion of the eastern Delta city of Pi-Ramasses to act as the forward supply base for Egyptian operations in the Levant.

In the spring of 1301 BC Ramasses led his army northwards to the Levant for the first time. Their passage along the Phoenician coast is traceable by the inscriptions he left at the ports of Tyre and Byblos. Reaching as far as Simyra, Ramasses then turned inland and attacked the kingdom of Amurru, a known vassal of the Hittites. With the Egyptian army at his gates and the Hittite army too far distant to offer support, Benteshina, the ruler of Amurru, had little choice but to inform Muwatallish that it was Ramasses II he now acknowledged as his suzerain. The pharaoh had now created the conditions for a future attack on Qadesh from two directions, one from the south through the Bekaa Valley and the other from Amurru itself. Both would be employed in the following year. The campaign complete, Ramasses and the army returned to Egypt with the young pharaoh greatly optimistic about the likelihood of regaining the 'lost' territories of central Syria in the following year.

## The Hittite response

There is no doubt that Muwatallish saw the Egyptian campaign as the first stage of a concerted attempt to recover their position in central Syria and thereafter extend their power into the north of the region. Unwilling to stand passively by and see the whole Hittite position in Syria demolished, Muwatallish resolved upon a strategy that would put paid to any further Egyptian aspirations in the region. The military campaign now planned for the following year identified two major tasks. Amurru was to be recovered; and the Egyptian army given such a trouncing that Ramasses would be denied the means to realise any of his wider political and territorial ambitions in the region.

It was clear many months before the battle took place that Qadesh would be the arena of contest. The Egyptians had contended ownership of the city with Mitanni and then Hatti since the days of Tuthmosis III. Such consistent and prolonged interest in the site arose naturally from its strategic position: not only was it the key to the Eleutheros Plain and therefore to Amurru, it was also the door to the Syrian Plain, and must be central to Ramasses' aspirations to extend Egyptian rule into northern Syria. It has also been suggested by a number of commentators that Qadesh was actually agreed upon in advance by the rival contestants as the venue for their battle, as indeed had the time. The existence of a measure of protocol concerning battles in the ancient period implies that prior agreement can be inferred by the proximity of the respective contestants at Qadesh at a particular time late in the month of May 1300 BC.

Notwithstanding, the site gave immense advantage to the Hittites. Muwatallish was operating in territory under Hittite control, supplied by loyal vassals and at the end of relatively short lines of communication, whereas the Egyptians would be operating some 1,600km from their home base. Furthermore, the city itself was large enough to accommodate the Hittite army should the battle go against them. It was also a very strongly fortified position, being enclosed by a moat and surrounded by the River Orontes itself.

*In this painted relief from Beit-al-Wali in Nubia a royal prince (possibly Ramasses II) leads representatives of conquered enemies into the presence of Seti I. Most are Syrians and Canaanites, although the one immediately to the rear of the prince is a Libyan. (British Museum)*

The army organised by the Hittite king was one of the largest ever assembled by the kingdom of Hatti. However, no document has come to light from that source detailing either its make-up or strength. All speculation concerning such matters must rest solely upon the details provided by the various Egyptian accounts of the Qadesh campaign (this and many other matters to do with the battle which cannot be explored here will be so in a forthcoming Osprey *Campaign* title). Ramasses speaks of the Hittites and their 18 allied and vassal states fielding as many as 3,700 chariots and 37,000 foot soldiers.

## Opening moves

Throughout the months of March and April the city of Pi–Ramasses became the assembly point for one of the largest armies ever raised by the Egyptians. Units were allocated to one of the four field armies (also referred to in the text as divisions). Noticeable was the increasing use of foreign troops in the regular army;

indeed this was to become even more marked in the centuries ahead. Apart from the Nubians and Sherden, Libyans and Canaanites were now in the employ of the standing army as mercenaries. The Egyptian character of the army was being diluted not just to increase manpower but also in pursuit of a deliberate policy to diversify the ethnic basis of the army as much as possible. The total strength of the Egyptian force was in the region of 20,000 men divided equally among the four field armies. Chariot strength is not given as a separate figure, but by this date the Egyptians must have been able to muster a very significant force.

Leaving Egypt at the end of April, the army took the coast road to Gaza, where Ramasses divided his forces. Turning inland with the bulk of his army, he followed the route through Canaan, traversing the eastern side of Lake Galilee and marching via the southern end of the Anti-Lebanon range and entering the Bekaa Valley to reach Kumidi. The smaller of the two forces, clearly an élite unit and one which was to play a decisive role in the battle, had been detached to advance northwards from Gaza along the coast road to Phoenicia. Their task was to ensure the loyalty of the Phoenician coastal cities by a show of force. However, their line of march from the coast was inland to bring them to Qadesh via the Eleutheros

*Only a fragment remains of the reliefs at Karnak detailing Seti I's second campaign in central Syria, in which he attacked the great city of Qadesh on the Orontes. The image shows the pharaoh's chariot trampling his enemies underfoot. Whatever the outcome of the attack, it is clear that by the end of his reign Qadesh lay squarely within the Hittite sphere of influence. (C. el Mahdy)*

Valley in Amurru. The pharaoh had no doubt impressed on their commander the need to arrive on a specific date, and therein lay their importance to Ramasses' strategy. It is clear when examining subsequent events that the Hittites were unaware of this detached unit.

Identified in the Qadesh inscriptions as simply the '*Ne'arin*', the question needs to be asked who exactly they were. The term itself means 'young men' and suggests that they were a crack Canaanite unit serving in the standing army and whose loyalty to Ramasses II was beyond question. It is most likely that they were

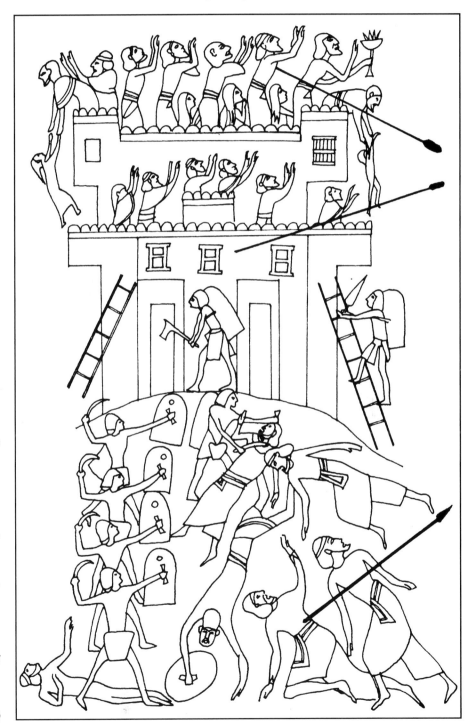

► *Egyptian siege methods of the period are well shown in this illustration in which the army of Ramasses II storms Ashkelon in southern Canaan; the artist depicts the different phases of the siege in one scene. At lower left the Egyptian battle line advances on the walls, clearing the enemy infantry. The attack on the city proper takes place with scaling ladders; the ascending infantry protect themselves with shields slung across their backs, while being given 'covering fire' by archers shooting at the battlements. Other troops attempt to cut through the city gates with their axes. (Firebird Books)*

*mariyannu* equipped as a well-armed flying column with chariots, chariot runners and other supporting infantry, able to traverse the greater distance to adesh and still reach the vicinity of the city on the appointed day. It is, however, of some interest that some commentators have suggested this unit was in fact the fourth army division named for Set.

Exactly one month after leaving Egypt Ramasses was encamped with the division of Amun on the morning of day 9 of the third month of Shemu (late May) on the Kamu'at el-Harmel ridge to the south of Qadesh. From this vantage point the valley lay ahead with the city itself in sight. At this point the other field armies—Re, Ptah and Set—lay to the rear of Amun along the line of march and separated by about one *iter* (about 10.5km), according to standard operating procedure. Striking camp, Ramasses and Amun descended from the ridge, traversed the forest of Labwi and began crossing the Orontes by the ford at Shabtuna. It was then that two Shasu-bedouin (whom it is generally assumed had been deliberately sent out by the Hittite king to misinform Ramasses) appeared and offered the information that Muwatallish and his army were nowhere near Qadesh, but in the land of Aleppo to the north of the city of Tunip, some 120 miles distant. If true, this would place Ramasses in a very strong position: he could collect his army, ensure that it was rested, and be ready for battle before the Hittites arrived. In short, he could do to them exactly what they intended to do to him.

*In about 1214 BC Seti I was obliged to take punitive action against Libyan tribes on the western border of Egypt. In this painted relief from Karnak he is seen in the classic triumphal pose, smiting the Libyans with his khopesh. Most are naked except for a leather phallus sheath; others wear a hide cloak as a measure of protection (see Plate F). (British Museum)*

confidence of the pharaoh was shared by the whole army and that its general conduct was remarkably tardy. Subsequent events may also serve to suggest that the army fielded by Ramasses II was of a lower quality than that deployed by Tuthmosis II at Megiddo, and that its professionalism was open to question. It seems that if such a reconnaissance had been carried out then the presence of Muwatallish and his large army in such close proximity to the east of Qadesh must have been detected.

As it was, Ramasses advanced forthwith. With the division of Amun he established camp slightly to the north-west of the city, in ignorance of the presence of the Hittites carefully screened on the far side of the Orontes. The division of Re was by now beginning to cross the Shabtuna ford (see map 1). While scouts might have been noticeable by their absence earlier, their activities now gave Ramasses his first intimation that all was far from well. Muwatallish, having received information that Ramasses was advancing on Qadesh from, in all likelihood, the very Shasu-bedouin who had misled Ramasses, despatched his own scouts to locate the pharaoh's exact position. It

Subsequent events can only be understood if we accept that Ramasses, through gullibility deriving from blind optimism and over-confidence, accepted this information without question. It would certainly seem that no reconnaissance was ordered as verification. If such was the case, then the outcome was a matter of absolute negligence. While historians frequently lay the blame at the feet of Ramasses, it is very hard to believe that the screening force of chariots or horsemen which normally moved ahead of the marching army were in this case absent. Such forces operated as a matter of course, and it would not have been the task of the pharaoh to order that such a normal operational procedure be carried out. If it was not absent, then it may well be that the over-

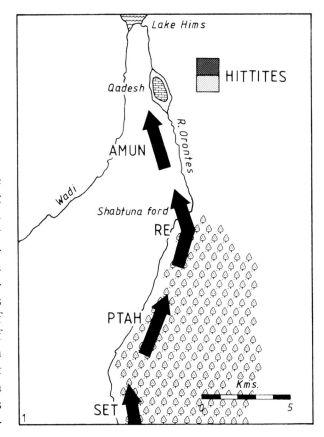

was two of these scouts whom their Egyptian counterparts now captured. Beaten, they were dragged in front of the pharaoh:

'Then said His Majesty, "What are you?" They replied, "We belong to the ruler of Hatti! He sent us out to see where Your Majesty was." Said His Majesty to them, "Where is he, the Ruler of Hatti? See, I heard it said that he was in the land of Aleppo, north of Tunip." They replied, "Behold, the Ruler of Hatti has already come, together with many foreign lands that he brought as allies … See, they are poised armed and ready to fight behind Old Qadesh?"'

### The battle

The reaction of the incredulous pharaoh was to call an immediate conference with his senior officers, the outcome of which was the despatch, post haste, of the vizier southwards to demand the rapid concentration of the divisions of Ptah and Set on Qadesh. Until their arrival Ramasses must depend on the power of the divisions of Amun and Re to resist any immediate Hittite attack. In this he was to be disappointed. As Re marched across the plain towards the camp of Amun, Muwatallish launched a major attack against the flank of the extended, marching division (map 2).

Emerging from dead ground and cover, a mighty host of Hittite chariotry poured across the Orontes to the immediate south of Qadesh itself and crashed into the flank of Re. The protective screen of Egyptian chariots was simply swept away by the sheer weight of the Hittite charge. While the exact size of the Hittite force is still a matter of great dispute, it is clear that it was sufficiently large to overwhelm the division of Re; however, it could not have approached in any way the vast figure of 2,500 chariots implied by Ramasses and seemingly quoted in such an uncritical fashion by so many commentators. The notion that a large Hittite detachment rather than the full chariot force was involved renders their rapid transit across the Orontes ford quite credible. It also places the 'single-handed' opposition of Ramasses later in the proceedings within the bounds of credibility as well.

With their own protective chariotry vanquished the cohesion of the Egyptian infantry companies—who were totally unprepared for combat—evaporated, and blind panic led to the disintegration of the whole of the division, with the survivors fleeing northwards towards the camp of Amun. From the vantage point of the camp of Amun the scene that now unfolded must have been desperate to behold. Behind the lines of fleeing infantry trying to reach the shield wall of Amun, huge numbers of Hittite chariots could be seen hurtling towards the camp, raising a wall of dust, their thousands of horses' hooves pounding the hard earth like thunder. Countless Egyptian infantry were ridden down or speared from behind by the chariot crews. The wave of panic then engulfed the camp of Amun, the defenders abandoning their positions and weapons as the Hittite chariotry broke in from the western side (map 3).

Watching the calamity from his own camp, which was set apart from that of Amun, Ramasses acted in perhaps the only way open to him if the rout was to be prevented from degenerating into a disaster. Donning his battle-armour, he mounted his chariot and prepared to go into action against the Hittite chariots virtually single-handed. Moving towards the enemy at speed, while at the same time appealing to his fleeing troops to rally, the pharaoh attacked the enemy with the assistance of perhaps only his immediate chariot-borne entourage. Launching themselves at

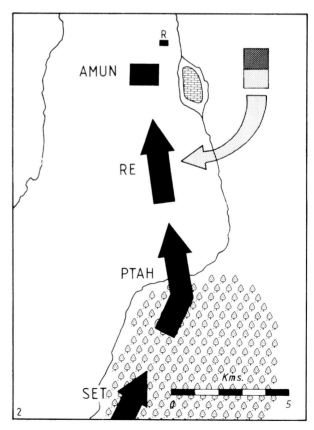

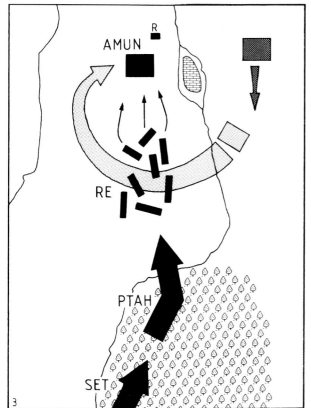

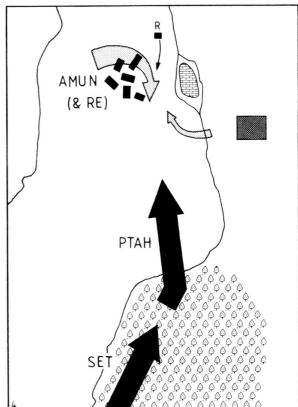

the Hittite eastern flank, the small numbers of Egyptian chariots proceeded to wreak havoc among the enemy, whose own cohesion and momentum was rapidly dissipating.

Utilising to the full the remarkable speed and manoeuvrability of the Egyptian chariots, Ramasses and his few supporters began to pick off the enemy in large numbers. With a ferocity born of desperation the pharaoh and his supporters attacked, turned and attacked again at least six times. In the swirling mêlée it is very possible that the Hittites were not aware of the small size of the force attacking them. From a vantage point overlooking the camp of Amun from across the river, Muwatallish could see how Ramasses was beginning to rectify the situation; and ordered a second wave of chariots across the river to support the first wave, who were now in trouble.

Once again we are faced with the problem of numbers. It is unlikely that the Hittite second wave contained as many as 1,000 chariots. Reaction time for Muwatallish was critical—he had to get chariots across the Orontes to attack Ramasses at once. He used those he had to hand, which in all likelihood

meant the aristocratic entourage who surrounded his person and who were sharing his view of the pharaoh's counterattack. They crossed the Orontes, but instead of making for Ramasses headed instead for his camp in the hope of distracting him from his harrying of the first group of Hittite chariots (map 4). However, the appearance on the scene at this moment of the *Ne'arin* prevented this. They attacked the Hittite reinforcements, and were later joined by Ramasses. In the subsequent contest few of the second wave of Hittite chariotry escaped back across the river (map 5); and many of those slain were of high rank from among the Hittite and allied states serving Muwatallish.

By the end of the day the pharaoh had managed to recoup the situation. The division of Amun was reassembled, and that of Ptah had also arrived at Qadesh by a forced march. In the aftermath of the battle it would seem that Ramasses may have visited grim punishment on many of his troops in the divisions of Amun and Re, who in his eyes had committed treason against his person by running away. According to some scholars there is evidence that on the

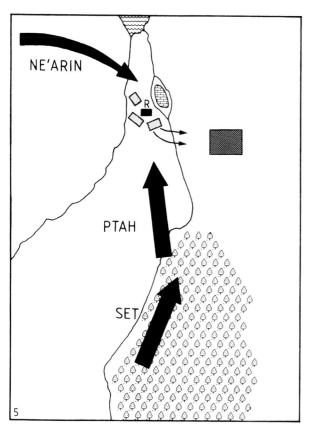

5

northern empire was swept away in the tide of human migration that covered the Near East at the beginning of the 12th century BC. By then, however, Ramasses II had already been in his grave for nearly 50 years.

# THE SEA PEOPLES

The death of the Pharaoh Merneptah in 1223 BC is a significant marker in the history of the New Kingdom, for thereafter Egyptian decline was very rapid. Merneptah had left a kingdom that in terms of size corresponded roughly to that of his father and was still outwardly powerful. Thereafter dynastic struggles characterised the closing years of the 19th Dynasty prior to the accession of Sethnakhte, the first pharaoh of the 20th Dynasty, in 1200 BC. His successor, Ramasses III, the last great pharaoh of the New Kingdom, saw the final disintegration of Egypt's empire in Canaan and the Levant as, along

day following the battle he ordered a decimation among his troops in full view of the Hittite king.

### Aftermath

An offer from the Hittite king of a military disengagement on the basis of peaceful co-existence was accepted by the pharaoh. While no hard and fast territorial demarcation followed, Ramasses never again campaigned in recognisably Hittite territory. Although he was engaged in Amurru some three years after Qadesh this was clearly not seen as a provocation by the Hittites, who by now had more immediate problems to face in the rise of Assyria on their eastern frontier and those territories to the north of Hatti.

It was in Year Twenty-One of Ramasses' reign that a formal treaty of peace was signed between Egypt and Hatti. Sealed by the marriage of the daughter of the Hittite king to Ramasses II, the treaty encompassed both a mutual defence pact and a formal demarcation of their respective territories in Syria. Whilst Ramasses was never to emulate Tuthmosis III, he inaugurated a treaty with the kingdom of Hatti that would be upheld by both powers until the great with the whole of the Near East, the region was convulsed by a mass invasion of dispossessed 'nations' known collectively as 'The Peoples of the Sea'.

Some of those identified by Ramasses III were already known to the Egyptians. In the fifth year of the reign of Merneptah (*c.* 1229 BC) a coalition of peoples attempted a mass invasion of Egypt from the west. They clearly came to settle, for they brought with them their families, their cattle and household possessions. Native North African tribes of old Egyptian acquaintance (notably the Libu, Meshwesh and Kehek) had allied themselves with others whose origin is thought to have been the coast and islands of the Aegean and Asia Minor. Those identified included the Sherden, Sheklesh, Lukka, Tursha and Akawasha. They had penetrated as far into Egypt as the Farafra oasis and the Canopic branch of the Nile before the pharaoh defeated them in battle.

The origin of the later wave of 'Sea Peoples' is thought to have been the same general area, although there is still much scholarly debate about the origins

of all of these ethnically diverse peoples. Ramasses III had to stop two further attempts at invasion from the west in 1193 and 1187 BC; but the most serious threat occurred in Year Eight of his reign, when the whole of the long-established political order of the Near East seemed to disintegrate: '... The foreign countries made a great conspiracy in their islands. All at once the lands were removed and scattered in the fray. No land could stand before their arms, from Hatti, Kode,

*The decisive encounter between Egypt and Hatti came in the reign of Ramasses II. In one of the most celebrated battles of the ancient world the young pharaoh and his army came perilously close to total disaster. In numerous reliefs at different sites in Egypt the pharaoh nevertheless left detailed accounts of the campaign. This scene, from the Luxor temple, shows Ramasses plunging into the mass of Hittite chariots and forcing them 'by the valour of his arm' to retreat back across the River Orontes, which loops round Qadesh itself. At the bottom of the picture Muwatallish stands with his infantry, impotent to intervene in the chariot battle on the other bank.*

Carchemish, Arzawa, and Alashiya, being cut off at one time. A camp was set up in a place in Amurru (the Lebanon). They desolated the people, and its land was like that which has never come into being. They were coming towards Egypt, while the flame was prepared before them. Their league was Peleset, Tjeker, Sheklesh, Denyen and Meshwesh, united lands.'

The Sea Peoples' advance on Egypt was by land and water. The observation made by Ramasses that 'this was certainly a great emergency and all had to go to the defence of their native land' picks up the observation made earlier about the level of call-up being as high as one in ten at this time. Clearly this invasion was perceived as a very great danger, on a scale the like of which had never threatened Egypt before. This *levée en masse* was clearly believed to be absolutely necessary. An initial line in southern Canaan manned by garrison troops and vassal *mariyannu* did not hold, for the main land drive by the Sea Peoples was almost certainly halted on the borders of Egypt itself. In the battle which now occurred the Egyptian line comprised infantry and chariots with support from Sherden auxiliaries. These are shown clashing with the enemy, some of whom are in Hittite-type three-man heavy chariots. The image of the invaders as a 'people on the move' is well conveyed on the walls of Medinet Habu by the way the Eygptians are seen fighting among the ox-drawn carts containing the women and children of the Sea Peoples.

The attack by sea, like that by land, was also routed. Ramasses states that the battle actually took place in the mouth of the Delta itself. The Egyptians seem to have mobilised every sort of craft: '. . . I caused the river mouth to be prepared like a strong wall with warships, transports and merchantmen, they were manned entirely from bow to stern with brave fighting men, and their weapons.' Once more the temple at Medinet Habu provides the visual

*It was in the twenty-first year of the reign of Ramasses II that the 'cold war' between Egypt and Hatti was ended by the signing of a peace treaty recognising a mutual frontier in Syria. The provisions also entailed a mutual defence pact, this being of no small significance to the Hittites, who were clearly perturbed by the rising power of Assyria on their eastern borders. Illustrated here is part of the copy of the treaty in Babylonian cuneiform, the diplomatic lingua franca of the age, discovered by archaeologists at the Hittite capital of Hattusas.*

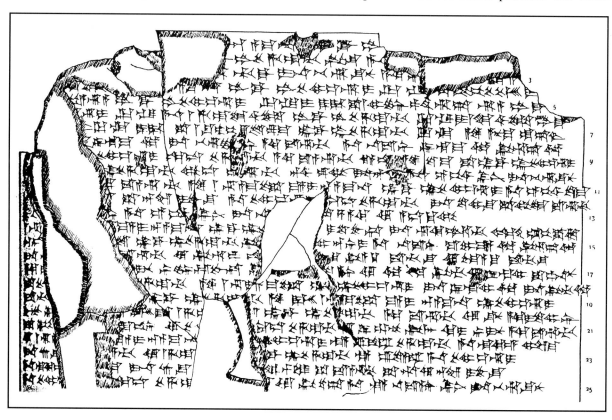

source for the battle. It is clear that the Egyptian ships planned to drive the enemy vessels close to the shore so that emplaced archers could rake the ships with arrows. For a more detailed account of this battle see the commentary on Plate J.

Despite the overwhelming victories claimed by Ramasses the mere fact that these invaders were able to settle in the coastal towns of Palestine is testimony to the impotence of Egypt to deny them. A little more than a century later the death of Ramasses XI brought to a close the 20th Dynasty, and with it the New Kingdom Period.

# THE PLATES

### A: Early New Kingdom Infantry
As with many other aspects of life in ancient Egypt, the continuity with the past is clearly seen in the appearance of these early New Kingdom infantry. Except for the acquisition of a number of new weapons like the bronze-headed axe and the *khopesh* sword, these three figures would not have been out of place in the Middle Kingdom period. Notwithstanding, the bulk of the armies of the pharaohs of the early 18th Dynasty would have comprised soldiers whose appearance would have been almost identical to those illustrated here. **A2** is a typical example of the close-combat infantry referred to as the *nakhtu-aa* or 'strong-arm boys'. All are devoid of any form of body protection, the only concession being the provision of a flap of stiffened linen material to cover the groin area, as in figure **A2**. **A1** and **A3** both carry the stave bow, the more complex and expensive composite bow having yet to filter down to the large numbers of archers in the infantry. **A3** is an example of the famous Medjay, extensively used by Kamose and Amosis in the war of liberation against the Hyksos as skirmishers and scouts. Later the term Medjay was used to designate their function as protectors of the royal tombs in the Valley of the Kings at Thebes.

### B: Early New Kingdom chariot and crew, c1430 BC
Until the reign of Tuthmosis IV (1425–1417 BC) Egyptian chariots had evolved little from those of the later Hyksos and Canaanite types that were their

The mummy of Pharaoh Merneptah (r.1236–23 BC). Although he bequeathed an empire to his successors almost as large as that of his father, he was nevertheless the last pharaoh of the New Kingdom to campaign in the old stamping grounds of the Levant. (C. el Mahdy)

models. They were characterised by four-spoked wheels and extreme lightness. Although this particular chariot draws upon an illustration from the tomb of Userhet, a royal scribe in the reign of Amenophis II, the following details are based upon a chariot of this period in the Museum of Florence. In profile the body of the vehicle is essentially an open wooden frame. Although the original material has not survived, the whole front of the cab extending to the lower sides would have been covered in leather. The height of the cab extended to about halfway up the thighs of the crew. They would have stood on a cab base made of leather thongs. The placement of the axle rod at the rear of the vehicle made it very stable and manoeuvrable. Analysis of the woods used in these chariots (such as elm for the pole, tyres of pine

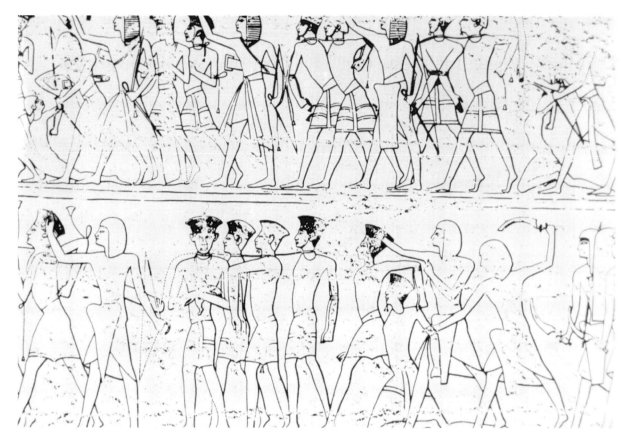

*It was on the borders of Egypt itself that Ramasses III defeated the attempted mass invasion by the 'Sea Peoples'. In this rendering from one of the reliefs on the temple walls at Medinet Habu Egyptian infantry round up and prepare to execute prisoners taken in the battle. Those in the lower rank are Denyen, Peleset and Tjekker; those with horned helmets are normally, although not exclusively identified as Sherden warriors. (C. el Mahdy)*

and birch for parts of the body) points to a need to import such materials from abroad, as they were not native to Egypt; that such woods came in quantity from the Levant perhaps explains, in part, the great exertions made by the pharaohs of the New Kingdom to control it. The horses used to pull these vehicles were small, one buried at Thebes being no more than about 12½ hands high.

Mitannian and Canaanite influence is very clearly discernible in the armour worn by the *seneny* or archer. The bronze corselet worn here was made of as many as 450 scales, although others with variable-size scales have many more; those of the best quality had smaller scales and many of them. Examples of scale

armour found in the palace of Amenophis III at Thebes are about 115mm in length and come to a point at the bottom. These scales were sewn onto an undergarment of leather or cloth. The weight of the armour was quite considerable and uncomfortable to wear, but such a price was worth paying for protection against the penetrating power of a composite bow. Around his neck the archer wears a heavy bronze collar; his helmet, also of bronze, is similar to that illustrated in Plate E. No Egyptian representation exists showing this panoply being worn in battle but much of this equipment may have been imported to Egypt as tribute. The *kedjen* or driver would have been poorly protected relative to the archer. The unfortunate Canaanite being ridden down is a typical peasant levy called up to support the *mariyannu* in battle.

### C: Enemies of Egypt: Mitanni

Although the Egyptians and Mitanni never met in a battle as momentous as that of Qadesh, it is clear that contact with them had a major impact on the Egyp-

*In a highly stylised image Ramasses III is portrayed presenting ranks of captive Sea Peoples to the gods Amun and Mut on the wall of the temple at Medinet Habu. The top line are identified as Sea People leaders, the middle row Denyen and the bottom Peleset—these being the forebears of the later Philistines.*

tians. Foremost among their military innovations was the *mariyannu*, a military aristocracy which in battle provided the cutting edge of the Hurri-Mitannian army. Illustrated here is an élite *mariyannu* chariot crew and their vehicle. Both wear heavy scale armour, the influence of which is clearly discernible in the Egyptian panoply in Plate B. The body armour of the archer comprises approximately 500 large scales for the body, 500 smaller scales for the arms, and about 200, smaller still, for the helmet. Such a panoply was very expensive to produce. He carries a powerful composite bow. The driver is equipped in more or less the same fashion, and carries a shield. Mitannian innovation can also be seen in the use of armour for the chariot cab and on the horse itself; the horse team illustrated here wears a scale armour 'coat'. The weapons complement of a Mitannian chariot comprised two bows, two quivers, a long spear and a chariot shield.

### D: Egyptian infantry despatching crew of Canaanite mariyannu chariot; reign of Seti I

Egyptian infantry began to change in appearance in the early 14th century BC with the introduction of a rudimentary form of body armour; the torso was now protected by stiffened textile bands, as was the unshielded shoulder. Helmets also begin to make their appearance among the infantry, as illustrated by D2; suggested materials for the helmet include textile, leather, or more probably—as shown here—bronze. Both men are wielding very long two-handed thrusting swords, the weapon measured about a metre, and was employed in its various guises throughout the 18th Dynasty. In this case the infantry are using their weapons to despatch the crew of a crashed Canaanite *mariyannu* chariot. Such soldiers would also have been employed in the garrisons in Canaan during the Amarna period.

The *mariyannu* of the time of Seti I rode chariots that were heavily influenced by Egyptian designs, although body armour, when worn, still reveals the influence of the kingdom of Mitanni. The *mariyannu* were always strong opposition for the Egyptians.

### E: Egyptian field musicians and standard bearers

For the manoeuvre of large formations on the battlefield the Egyptians relied upon the passing of signals by war trumpets. Although they were only capable of producing a few basic notes, these were clearly keyed to instructions such as 'advance', 'retreat', etc. As in other armies down through history, the drums would no doubt have accompanied the infantry into battle, dictating their rate of advance, as well as being employed in more pacific tasks such as accompanying marching troops on parade. It is known that entry into battle by the Egyptians was accompanied by much noise from the instruments as well as from the battlecries and songs of the troops.

Standards in the Egyptian army ranged from those

employed at the head of the field armies representing the gods Amun, Re, Ptah and Set (in the time of Ramasses II) to those carried by the standard bearers in the chariot and infantry units. As in all armies such tokens fulfilled a number of roles. Clearly, unit identification on the battlefield was necessary for command and control; the standard was also important to unit morale and status. That carried in the bearer and numbered E4 is an animal motif, exact meaning uncertain. E5 is an ostrich plume carried by the chariotry and high-ranking officers, E6 a common fan standard, and E7 the war god Montu.

### F: 19th-Dynasty infantry in battle with Libyans

By the early 19th Dynasty Egyptian close-combat troops had acquired the appearance that was to last until the end of the New Kingdom. A distinguishing feature of infantry of this period which sets them apart from those of the 18th Dynasty is the striped headcloth. The shield has become larger and more rectangular than that shown in Plate D, and allowed infantry bodies to present a 'shield wall' when necessary. Many reliefs from the period show these shields slung across the backs of infantry either on the march or in battle, particularly when two hands were needed to wield the mace axe, as F2 is doing. The shields were also slung across the back when ascending scaling ladders in a siege. Other weapons carried by infantry include the bronze *khopesh*, which by this period had become large and very formidable. Individuals would also have employed throwsticks as a matter of preference.

Throughout the 19th Dynasty the Egyptians had to deal with irruptions across their western borders by Libyan tribes. As can be seen, attire of any sort was minimal; most Libyan warriors wore nothing except tattoos and a leather phallic sheath. The hair was normally arranged and decorated with ostrich plumes which may have indicated status. When clothing of any sort was worn it was normally in the form of a hide cloak that functioned as a body protector. Significantly, the warrior shown as F4 wields a sword acquired from the 'Sea Peoples' and very similar to those used by the Sherden employed by Ramasses II.

### G: Late New Kingdom chariot, reign of Ramasses II

Compared to that in Plate B, this chariot shows a

The sea battle at the mouth of the Nile took place after the invaders had been defeated on land. These two illustrations pick out the detail of the Egyptian and Sea Peoples' warships, and are again from Medinet Habu. The original illustrations provide the inspiration for our Plate J.

number of significant differences that illustrate the way the Egyptians responded to the technical challenges posed by their enemies. The three most significant features were the adoption of a six-spoked wheel, a heavier cab and armour for the horses. The switch from four to six spokes can be dated to the reign of Tuthmosis IV, and occurred as a consequence of the growth in weight of the cab as it too became stronger to carry the heavier armoured crew and greater weaponry needed to contest with the heavier Hittite chariots. Eight-spoked wheels were tried at the beginning of the 14th century BC, but six spokes became the norm thereafter. The horse armour arose out of the need to protect the team from missiles targeted specifically at them; for an archer in a chariot approaching an enemy vehicle at full tilt the horses made a far larger target than the crew, and wounding or killing a horse would in all likelihood cause the chariot to crash. The task of disposing of or capturing the crew would be left to the chariot runners (G3), who followed their own vehicles into battle. While the driver G1 wears textile armour and carries a shield, the archer G2 is dressed in a scale corselet with the scales stitched to a textile undergarment. Compared with that worn by the charioteer in Plate B this armour would have been much lighter, but nevertheless strong and effective. The relative comfort of this lighter panoply would no doubt have been most welcome in the high temperatures of the Near East. The 'helmet' would have been made in the same manner as the corselet.

## H: Later New Kingdom archers, and mounted messenger

By the Ramasside period (19th and 20th Dynasties) archers were wholly equipped with the composite bow. The standard Egyptian tactic of employing massed firepower would now have had an even more devastating effect on the battlefield. That archers were still not expected to close with the enemy is evidenced by their general lack of body armour, although a number of reliefs show archers wearing striped jerkins that on other figures are assumed to represent scale armour. H1 dates from the reign of Ramasses III and is based upon a relief at the temple of Medinet Habu.

Although the Egyptians did not employ battlefield cavalry, it is clear that horsemen nevertheless fulfilled

a number of important tasks. They were employed essentially to carry messages from one part of the battlefield to another, and also for forward reconnaissance. Protection is provided by a form of textile armour.

## I: Enemies of Egypt: the Hittites

Notwithstanding the pejorative labelling of Hittite soldiers as *humty* or 'women-soldiers' by Ramasses II, on account of the way they wore their hair, it is clear that the Egyptians found them very formidable opponents. It is also clear that guile and ingenuity played as great a role in their military expertise as did the quality of their army; indeed, the near-destruction of the Egyptian army at Qadesh is testimony to that. Illustrated here is the three-man chariot, the primary offensive weapon of the Hittite army. The major sources for the appearance of these vehicles are the Qadesh reliefs of Ramasses II, which clearly detail the variety of types employed, reflecting that for this battle Muwatallish deployed chariots belonging to vassals and many states allied to Hatti. That illustrated here has its cab made of wood and, unlike the Egyptian types, has its axle mounted mid-way along the body. Whilst many of the Qadesh reliefs show horses lacking armour, other sources do show it being worn and in a style similar to that formally employed by Mitanni. That around the body is bronze scale armour, while the covering around the head is studded fabric.

The crew illustrated here comprises a driver, shield bearer and armoured spearman. The first two wear lightweight textile armour, the latter a bronze helmet and scale body armour. The distinctive Hittite shields shown here are clearly to be seen on the Qadesh reliefs. Although the kingdom of Hatti was ultimately to be swept away by the Sea Peoples in about 1190 BC the reliefs of Ramasses III are clear in detailing Hittite-type three-man chariots in the land battle on the border of Egypt. Where possible the Egyptians would attempt to use the superior speed and manoeuvrability of their own chariots to avoid close combat with those of the Hittites. However, if the Hittites caught the Egyptian chariotry off guard the sheer momentum of their heavier vehicles may well have been decisive. It is precisely this situation which led to the rout of the division of Re at Qadesh. Caught on the march and unable to manoeuvre the

Egyptian chariots were swamped by their heavier Hittite counterparts.

## J: The naval battle with the Sea Peoples; c1190 BC

Although Ramasses III stated on his inscriptions at Medinet Habu that boats of many types were mobilised to contest the Sea Peoples' attack on the mouth of the Nile, those Egyptian vessels that actually fought in the battle were clearly warships. While the Sea Peoples' ships are depicted without oars it is clear that they must have had them: their simple square sail meant that they were unable to tack, and was therefore a supplement to the oars rather than a substitute for them. The Egyptian artist may have depicted the enemy vessels without oars because in combat they would have been shipped, since the oarsmen, unlike their Egyptian equivalents, doubled as fighting men. The Sea Peoples' double-ended ships with the bird's head at the prow were probably much less manoeuvrable in battle than the Egyptian vessels. Indeed, the reliefs illustrate one Egyptian vessel back-sculling as a grapnel line snagged in the enemy rigging is pulled backwards in order to capsize the vessel.

Even allowing for the propagandist nature of the Medinet Habu reliefs it is clear that the Egyptians inflicted fearful casualties on the Sea Peoples with their composite bows, given the very large number of dead bodies depicted in the water. Noticeable by their absence are any bows among the enemy crews. It was therefore a major tactic for the Egyptians to stand off, and in this action they were helped by archers operating from land; the Egyptians herded the Sea Peoples' vessels close in shore to allow the archers on the beach to add their firepower to that of shipborne archers.

## K: The Sea Peoples' land invasion

It is clear from inscriptions describing the land fighting against the Sea Peoples that the invasion of Egypt was carried out by whole communities and not just by warriors. The reliefs graphically depict Egyptian troops fighting their enemies among ox-drawn carts carrying not only soldiers, but women and children as well. We can only surmise that in stopping this human tide the Egyptians inflicted heavy loss on the invaders. Nevertheless, their recoil into Canaan left them sufficiently strong to occupy the coastline of Palestine and deny those territories to the Egyptians. While Ramasses III was able to record, in appropriately bombastic fashion, his defeat of the Sea Peoples on the walls of the temple at Medinet Habu, the event itself is the last great military success of New Kingdom Egypt. In the years that followed, the decline of the former great power was very swift, and terminal.

---

Notes sur les planches en couleur

A A l'exception de certaines armes nouvelles que ces personnages ont acquises, comme la hache à tête de bronze et l'épée khopesh, leur apparence n'aurait pas été déplacée pendant la période du Moyen Empire. A2 est un exemple typique de l'infanterie de combat rapproché ou nakhtu-aa. A1 et A3 portent l'arc à hampe, l'arc composite plus complexe et plus cher n'ayant pas encore infiltré les nombreux rangs des archers d'infanterie. A3 est un exemple des célèbres Medjay qui servirent en grand nombre dans la querre de libération contre les Hyksos comme éclaireurs et provocateurs d'escarmouches. Aucun de ces personnages ne portait de protection à l'exception d'un rabat de toile raidie pour se couvrir l'aine.

B Char égyptien dont le modèle s'inspire des types récents Hyksos et cananéen. Caractérisé par des roues à quatre rayons et son extrême légèreté. Vu de profil, ce véhicule est essentiellement une structure de bois ouverte.' Toute la voiture et les pans inférieurs auraient été couverts de cuir. L'équipage se tenait sur une base faite de lanières de cuir tandis que la position de l'essieu à l'arrière donnait une grande stabilité et manoeuvrabilité au char. L'archer ou seneny montre clairement une influence mitannienne ou cananéenne. Il porte un corselet de bronze, un lourd col et un casque de bronz également. Comparé à l'archer, le pilote ou kedjen est beaucoup peu protégé. Les Cananéens formaient les rangs des recrues paysannes.

C L'equipage d'élite ou mariyannu d'un char et leur véhicule. Les deux membres de l'équipage portent une lourde armure d'écailles dont l'influence se reconnaît dans la panopile égyptienne de la gravure B. L'archer porte un arc composite, puissant. Le pilote est équipé plus ou moins de la même manière et porte un bouclier. Une armure de cette nature coûtait fort cher à produire. L'innovation mitannienne se voit dans l'utilisation de la cuirasse couvrant la voiture et le cheval. Les armes complétant un char mitannien comprenaient deux arcs, deux carquois, une longue lance et un bouclier de char.

D Au début de XIVe siècle av. JC, l'aspect de l'infanterie commença à changer avec l'introduction d'une armure rudimentaire couvrant le corps. Le torse est alors protégé par des bandes rigides de même que les épaules sans armure. D2 présente un exemple des casques qui commencèrent à apparaître parmi l'infanterie. Les deux hommes utilisent de très longues épées d'estoc qui se portaient des deux mains. Les

Farbtafeln

A Mit Ausnahme bestimmter neuer Waffen, die diese Gestalten erhalten haben, wie etwa die Axt mit dem Bronzekopf und das Kopesh-Schwert, würden diese Krieger auch im Mittleren Reich nicht auffallen. A2 Ein typisches Beispiel für Nahkampf-Infanterie, mit der Bezeichnung Nakhtu-aa. A1 und A2 tragen Stegbogen, das sind komplexere und kostspieligere zusammengesetzte Bogen, die bis jetzt noch nicht bis zur grossen Masse der Fussvolk-Bogenschützen gelangt sind. A3 Ein Beispiel für die berühmten Medjay, die im Befreiungskampf gegen die Hyksos weithin als Kundschafter und Plänkler eingesetzt wurden. Keiner von ihnen trägt irgendeine Art von Rüstung, mit Ausnahme einer Art von Lendenschurz aus versteiftem Leinenmaterial.

B Streitwagen ägyptischer Art nach dem Muster der später von den Hyksos und Kanaanitern verwendeten. Gekennzeichnet durch vierspeichige Räder und aussergewöhnliche Leichtigkeit. Im Profil ist der Wagen im Grunde ein offener Holzrahmen; Die ganze Vorderseite und die niedrigeren Seiten waren lederbespannt. Die Besatzung stand auf einer aus Lederriemen bestehenden Basis, und die Anbringung der Achse an der Hinterseite verleih dem Streitwagen hohe Stabilität und Manövrierfähigkeit. Der Bogenschütze oder Seneny zeigt deutlich mitannische oder kanaanitische Einflüsse. Er trägt einen Harnisch aus Bronze und einen schweren Halskragen und Helm aus dem gleichen Material. Verglichen mit ihm ist der Fahrer des Streitwagens, der Kedjen, nur sehr wenig geschützt. Der Kanaaniter ist typisch für die in den Militärdienst gepressten Bauern.

C Eine elitäre Mariyannu-Streitwagenbesatzung samt dem Fahrzeug. Beide Männer tragen schwere Schuppenpanzer, deren Einfluss bei der ägyptischen Rüstung in Tafel B erkennbar ist. Der Bogenschütze trägt den leistungsstarken zusammengesetzten Bogen. Der lenker ist mehr oder weniger auf gleiche Weise ausgerüstet und trägt noch keinen Schild. Rüstung wie diese waren in der Herstellung höchst kostspielig. Die mitannischen Neuerungen zeigen sich in der Verwendung einer Panzerung des Streitwagens und des Pferdes. Dei Bewaffnung eines mitannischen Streitwagens bestand aus zwei Bogen, zwei Köchern, einem langen Speer und einem Streitwagen-Schild.

D Im frühen 14. Jahrhundert v.Chr. veränderte sich das Aussehen des ägyptischen mariyannu montaient des chars montrant une forte influence égyptienne mais leur armure révèle toujours l'influence mitannienne.

**E** Les Egyptiens utilisaient des trompettes de guerre pour aider à manoeuvrer de grandes formations sur le champ de bataille. Bien qu'elles ne puissent jouer que quelques notes, elles étaient accordées pour donner des instructions telles que "avancée", "retraite", etc. Des tambours accompagnaient également l'infanterie à la bataille dictant la vitesse d'avance et servant également lors des défilés. L'avance égyptienne pendant la bataille se faisait à grand bruit créé par le son des instruments, des chants et des cris. Les étendards de l'armée égyptienne allaient de ceux des armées à ceux des unités individuelles. **E4** un motif d'animal dont la signification est incertaine. **E5** une plume d'autruche portée par les chars de guerre et les officiers de haut rang et **E6** un étendard courant en forme d'éventail. **E7** le dieu Montu de la guerre.

**F** l'infanterie de combat rapproché telle qu'elle apparaîtra jusqu'à la fin de la période du Nouvel Empire. Un trait caractéristique de cette période est le foulard rayé porté sur la tête. Le bouclier est devenu plus grand et plus rectangulaire pour permettre aux corps de l'infanterie de présenter un mur de bouclier lorsque c'était nécessaire. Lorsqu'ils escaladaient les échelles de siège ou maniaient des armes à deux mains, le bouclier était souvent rejeté dans le dos comme sur la gravure **F2**. Parmi les autres armes portées par les fantassins, les batons de lancer et les formidables khopesh vu leur dimension maintenant. Les Libyens portaient un minimum de vêtements, la plupart d'entre eux rien d'autre que des tatouages et une gaine de cuivre couvrant le sexe. La chevelure était généralement arrangée et décorée de plumes d'autruche qui indiquaient peut-être le rang. S'ils portaient un vêtement, c'était généralement une cape de cuir. **F4** manoeuvre une épée acquise auprès des "Hommes de la Mer".

**G** Un char plus lourd avec roues à six rayons, une partie de voiture plus lourde et une cuirasse pour les chevaux en vue de lutter contre les chars hittites plus lourds. La cuirasse du cheval est née du besoin de protection de l'attelage contre les projectiles le visant spécifiquement. Lorsqu'un cheval de char lancé à fond de train bombait, selon toute probabilité le char s'évrasait. Le pilote porte une armure en toile et un bouclier tandis que l'archer porte le **G2** un gilet d'écailles. Cette armure aurait été plus légère que celle de la gravure B mais néanmoins résistante et efficace. Le casque est en écailles cousues sur une pièce de tissu de la même manière que le corselet.

**H** A cette période, tous les archers étaient équipés d'un arc composite, ce qui augmentait fortement l'effet de la tactique égyptienne courante de tir groupé. Les témoignages continuent à montrer clairement que les archers ne firent pas partie des troupes de combat rapproché, vu bien que le manque d'armure protégeant le corps, bien que certaines illustrations montrent une forme de protection. Les Egyptiens n'employaient pas de cavalerie sur le champ de bataille mais utilisaient néanmoins des cavaliers pour les tâches de reconnaissance et pour porter les messages. Ils sont protégés par une armure de toile.

**I** Un char à trois combattants qui fut l'arme principale d'offensive de l'armée hittite. La source principale en ce qui concerne l'aspect de ces véhicules provient des reliefs de Kadesh de Ramsès II. Ceux-ci montrent clairement que lors de la bataille de Kadesh Muwatallish déploya des chars appartenant à ses vassaux et à de nombreux Etats alliés de Hatti. Celui illustré a une voiture de bois et un essieu monté à mi-chemin le long de la carrosserie, contrairement aux chars égyptiens. Alors que de nombreux reliefs de Kadesh présentent des chevaux sans cuirasses, d'autres les montrent avec cuirasse dans un style semblable à celui des Mitanniens. Le corps est couvert d'une armure en écailles de bronze tandis que une tête est protégée par un tissu garni de clous. L'équipage consistait d'un pilote et d'un écuyer tout deux protégés par une légère armure et d'un homme armé d'une lance et portant une armure complète avec casque de bronze et armure d'écailles couvrant le corps.

**J** Les bateaux des "Hommes de la Mer" sont dépeints sans rames mais il est quasiment certain qu'ils en portaient. Ils étaient expédiés à la bataille et leurs équipages venaient doubler les rangs des combattants, contrairement à leurs homologues égyptiens. Leurs bateaux étaient probablement moins manoeuvrables en bataille que ceux des Egyptiens et ce fait associé à leur manque apparent d'arcs les rendaient vulnérables aux archers égyptiens. Il est clair d'après le nombre de corps dépeint dans l'eau que les Egyptiens infligèrent des pertes terribles à ces "Hommes de la Mer".

**K** Il est clair d'après les inscriptions décrivant les combats terrestres contre les "Hommes de la Mer" que l'invasion de l'Egypte fut menée par des communautés entières et non pas seulement par des guerriers. Les reliefs montrent les troupes égyptiennes combattant leurs ennemis parmi des chars à boeuf transportant non seulement des soldats mais aussi des femmes et des enfants. Bien qu'il soit probable que les Egyptiens aient infligé de lourdes pertes en repoussant cette invasion, les "Hommes de la Mer" conservèrent des forces suffisantes pour occuper la côte de la Palestine et interdire l'accès à ces territoires aux Egyptiens.

Fussvolks mit der Einführung einer rudimentären Rüstung. Der Torso war jetzt durch versteifte Bänder geschützt, ebenso der Arm, der keinen Schild trug. **D2** Ein Beispiel für die Helme, die jetzt beim Fussvolk langsam Einzug hielten. Beide Männer tragen lange, zweihändige Stechschwerter. Die Mariyannu fuhren auf Streitwagen, die stark von der ägyptischen Konstruktion beeinflusst waren, während ihre Rüstunge immer noch den mitannischen Einfluss erkennen lassen.

**E** Die Agypter verwendeten Kriegstrompeten, um das Manövrieren grosser Truppenformationen auf dem Schlachtfeld zu erleichtern. Obwohl diese Trompeten nur einen Bereich von wenigen Noten hatten, waren sie doch auf Kommandos wie "Vormarsch", "Rückzug" usw. abgestimmt. Auch Trommeln begleiteten das Fussvolk ins Gefecht, um das Tempo des Vormarsches anzugeben; sie wurden aber auch bei Paraden benutzt. Der ägyptische Vormarsch ins Gefecht wurde sehr lautstark nicht nur von den erwähnten Instrumenten sondern auch von Gesängen und Schlachtrufen begleitet. Die Standarten der ägyptischen Armee reichten von solchen für ganze Armee bis zu den Standarten der einzelnen Einheiten. **E4** Ein Tiermotiv, dessen genaue Bedeutung ungewiss ist. **E5** Eine Straussenfeder, wie sie Streitwagenbesatzungen und hohe Offiziere trugen. **E6** Eine gewöhnliche Fächer-Standarte. **E7** Der Kriegsgott Montu.

**F** Nahkampf-Fussvolk, wie es bis zum Ende des Neuen Reiches aussah. Typisch für diese Periode ist das gestreifte Kopftuch. Der Dchild ist grösser und rechteckiger geworden, so dass die Infanterie im Bedarfsfalle einen Schildwall bilden konnte. Beim Erklettern von Mauerleitern oder beim beidhändigen Schwingen des Schwertes hing der Schild oft auf dem Rücken, siehe **F2**. Andere Infanteriewaffen waren schleuderstöcke und das Khopesh-Schwert, das inzwischen gross und beeindruckend geworden war. Die Libyer trugen nur ein Minimum an Kleidung – meistens nicht mehr als Tätowierungen und einen ledernen Phallus-Schutz. Das Haar war meist mit Straussenfedern geschmückt, die individuellen Rang angezeigt haben dürften. Wurde überhaupt Kleidung getragen, dann war es meist ein Lederumhang. **F4** trägt ein Schwert, das von den "Meervölkern herkommt".

**G** Ein schwererer Streitwagen mit sechsspeichigen Rädern und Panzer für die Pferde; konstruiert, um gegen die schwereren Streitwagen der Hittiter bestehen zu können. Der Pferdepanzer erwuchs aus der Notwendigkeit, das Gespann vor speziell gegen die Pferde gezielten Geschossen zu schützen. Wenn ein Pferd im vollen Lauf durch Pfeile oder Lanzen zum Sturz kam, hätte das zweifellos auch den ganzen Streitwagen zu Fall gebracht. Der Lenker **G1** trägt eine Stoffrüstung, während der Lenker **G2** ein Schuppenwams trägt. Dieser Panzer war leichter als der in Tafel B, aber trotzdem fest und wirksam. Der Helm besteht aus Schuppen, die auf eine Stoffunterlage aufgenäht sind, ähnlich wie der Brustharnisch.

**H** In dieser Periode waren die Bogenschützen bereits alle mit dem zusammengesetzten Bogen ausgerüste, der die typische ägyptische Taktik des massierten Pfeilbeschusses wesentlich wirksamer machte. Dass aber die Bogenschützen keine Nahkampftruppen waren, zeigt sich immer noch deutlich das allgemeine Fahlen von Rüstungen, wenn auch manche Abbildungen gewisse Formen von Körperschutz zeigen. Eine ägyptische Kavallerie auf dem Schlachtfeld gab es nicht, doch wurden Reiter für Erkundungen und als Boten eingesetzt. Schutz wurde durch eine Art von Stoffrüstung geboten.

**I** Ein Drei-Mann-Streitwagen – die primäre Angriffswaffe der Hittiter. Hauptquelle für das Erscheinen dieser Wagen sind die Kadesh-Reliefs von Ramses II., die deutlich zeigen, dass Muwatallish in dieser Schlacht Streitwagen benutzte, die Vasallen und anderen Verbündeten der Hittiter gehörten. Der hier abgebildete Streitwagen hat einen Holzkörper, entlang dem die Achse in der Mitte montiert ist, anders als bei dem ägyptischen Gegenstück. Während viele Kadesh-Reliefs ungepanzerte Pferde zeigen, zeigen andere Pferde, die ähnlich denen der Mitanni gepanzert sind. Der Körper ist von einem Schuppenpanzer bedeckt, der Kopf durch ein beschlagenes Tuch. Die Besatzung besteht aus einem Lenker und einem Schildträger, beide mit leichten Stoffrüstungen, und aus einem gepanzerten Speerträger mit Bronzehelm und Schuppenpanzer.

**J** Die Schiffe der "Meeresvölker" sind ohne Ruder abgebildet, die sie aber fast sicher mitgeführt haben; sie wurden jedoch im Gefecht eingezogen, und die Ruderer setzten dann mit, im Gegensatz zu ihren ägyptischen Kollegen. Ihre Schiffe waren wahrscheinlich weniger manövrierfähig als die ägyptischen, wodurch sie zusammen mit dem anscheinenden Fehlen von Bogen sehr verwundbar durch die ägyptischen Bogenschützen waren. Nach der hier abgebildeten grossen Anzahl von Leichen im Wasser zu schliessen, dürften die ägyptischen Schiffe ihren Gegnern schwere Verluste beigebracht haben.

**K** Aus inschriften, in denen die Landgefechte gegen die "Meervölker" beschrieben werden, geht klar hervor, dass die Invasion Agyptens von ganzen Gemeinschaften und nicht nur von Soldaten durchgeführt wurde. Die Reliefs zeigen ägyptische Truppen im Kampf inmitten von Ochsen gezogenen Karren, die nicht nur Soldaten, sondern auch Frauen und Kinder trugen. Obwohl es wahrscheinlich ist, dass die ägyptische Armee bei Abweisung dieser Invasion den Gegnern schwere Verluste beibrachte, blieben die "Meeresvölker" doch noch stark genug, um die palästinensische Küste zu besetzen und diese Territorien gegen ägyptische Angriffe zu behaupten.